INSIDE
THE OTHER
SIDE

Also by Concetta Bertoldi

Do Dead People Walk Their Dogs?
Do Dead People Watch You Shower?

INSIDE THE OTHER SIDE

SIDE

SOUL CONTRACTS, LIFE LESSONS, AND HOW DEAD PEOPLE HELP US, BETWEEN HERE AND HEAVEN

CONCETTA BERTOLDI

WILLIAM MORROW

An Imprint of HarperCollinsPublishers

HarperCollins books may be purchased for educational, business, or sales promotional use. For information please write: Special Markets Department, HarperCollins Publishers, 10 East 53rd Street, New York, NY 10022.

FIRST EDITION

Designed by Diahann Sturge

Library of Congress Cataloging-in-Publication Data has been applied for.

ISBN 978-0-06-208740-9

12 13 14 15 16   OV/RRD   10 9 8 7 6 5 4 3 2 1

This book is dedicated to my friend and sister Cornelia DiNunzio (a.k.a. Mushy). We met as young girls, at the tender age of nine. After all these years I can only say I am grateful for the Soul Link Group we were born into. You have amazed me throughout our lives with your talents, and I could write a very interesting book about our relationship alone. There are those who tried to come between us, but our love for each other has always prevailed. I love you from the bottom of my heart. Thank you, my darling girl, for everything you have unselfishly given me.

Contents

It's Not the End of the World

Over the past decade or so I've been hearing among many of my clients increasing concerns about the year 2012, when, according to some interpretations of the Mayan calendar, the world is supposed to come to an end. This is simply not the case. Twenty twelve could be looked at more as a kind of tipping point for a huge change that has been taking place gradually over many years. I could compare it somewhat to when we moved from the Piscean Age to the Aquarian Age—for decades this change was anticipated and celebrated and lots of people studied what could be expected in such a new time. For most of us it was an exciting time to look forward to being a part of. But nothing of this nature happens in a blink. Changes in the cosmos, on earth, and in people's minds and behaviors happen gradually, over time.

Our world is not ending; we are now in the process of creating a new one. I've been hearing it from my coworkers, the souls on the Other Side, for a long time now. And I see it all around me, in spite of all the terrible things appearing on the news all the time— I'm not going to try to convince anyone that life on planet Earth is not tough! People are gradually opening up—if we could see this from a bird's-eye view, speeded up, it might be like watching time-lapse photography of a flower blooming. Attitudes are changing. People are waking up. They're trying to repair and restore our environment and change their damaging behaviors, both on a personal level and on a global level. Science is finding ways of preventing or curing the diseases that have caused grief to so many over the years and working out new and better ways for us to live our lives. Minds are opening in regard to the differences between us. We still have a long way to go in all of this, but in my lifetime I've seen a tremendous amount of change on these and so many other fronts. For me personally it's been exciting to see folks get more interested in learning about the spiritual side of life—once so shrouded in fear and misunderstanding—and acknowledge its reality and importance in their lives.

But even as life on earth goes on, as a psychic medium, so much of my daily work centers around clients who come to me in true despair, feeling like their own life is ending. They've lost someone who was dear to them and sometimes feel like they can't go on without that person beside them here. Often they want to hear that their loved one is safely home and at peace—they tell me they want closure. And I hope that when they leave my office they feel that this has been accomplished. But I don't think that providing closure is the most important aspect of my work. What I feel is more important to convey is that their loved one who has crossed is still very much with them and will always be—watching over them, loving them, assisting them in any way possible on this very difficult journey we each are making on this side of the veil.

Every one of us struggles here. Hardly anyone believes they have a dream family, perfect health, a true friend, a true love, true prosperity. Even if we come from a big family or are in a serious relationship, so often we feel like we're alone. This sense of separateness, aloneness, is actually a conundrum of this side of the veil—it's both real and an illusion. Here, in physical form, each of us is in a way separate and each of us is here on our own journey, for our own purpose. At the same time we are truly spirits, all of us are one, with one universal goal and purpose—simply to be God's love.

This is the side they call the "vale of tears." This side is the fire that tempers and tries every soul—it's where we meet our challenges, learn our lessons, learn to love. Nobody can do it for us and yet the spiritual truth is that everybody is here to help us— whether on this side or the Other Side. No one is alone. We are all one.

What we know as physical life and death are on a continuum, a cycle, a wheel. Every day the world appears to end for someone and begins for someone else as a baby is born. Yet we never really leave or lose connection with each other since the Other Side is right here. In spirit, those who have "died" in the body are still with us. We still have their love and we can give them ours.

There have always been people predicting the end of the world. Back in 2011 there was a radio preacher in California who told everyone that the world would end May 21 of that year. Thousands of people believed this and I assume got their lives in order— not that it would matter really if there was no one left here to see that they hadn't folded their laundry before leaving. Of course the world didn't end so this preacher told everyone he'd messed up his calculations and the world was really going to end in October. We're still here, and he's going to have to keep on recalculating because I don't think we're going anywhere any time soon.

Sometimes we really get the rug pulled out from under us and it can take a while to get back on our feet, but life goes on. Twenty twelve won't be the end of the world; neither will getting downsized, getting sick, wrecking a relationship, or even, I say with great sympathy, seeing the one dearest to you pass from this life. Life goes on and we must go on with it. But when you're down so low the street curb looks high, you may need a bit of assistance to learn how to live again. Ironically, that's where the dead guys come in. Every single one of us receives help from the Other Side and that's what this book is about.

Relief for our grief is *believing*.

A lot of people like to say that seeing is believing. I like to say that *believing* is *seeing*.

A Few Words About the Way It All Works . . .

> Death is not extinguishing the light, it is only putting out
> the lamp because the dawn has come.
>
> —Rabindranath Tagore

A while back I was talking with a psychologist friend. He'd asked me to explain how I'm able to connect with and listen to dead people. After I told him he said, "You know, you're just like a schizophrenic. At the top of your consciousness, both you and the schizophrenic have got holes in the roof. The only difference is that you are able to control what voices come in through the holes and the schizophrenic can't."

Nice.

The reality is that the spirits of our loved ones who have crossed to the Other Side are with us all the time. But most people, I guess, have fewer holes in the roof—that is, they're not as tuned in to this reality as a psychic medium is—so those voices aren't getting through to their consciousness. For most, I realize, connecting with the spirit of someone no longer "alive" in physical form is a pretty strange thing. And even though I've been hearing from the dead my entire life and I've done readings for thousands of people both privately and at my larger shows, I'm well aware that there are some who do not believe this is possible. So it's probably important to say a little bit about how this all works before we get into other subjects.

I've heard dead guys talking to me since I was a young child—it's an ability that I just happen to have so I always find it challenging to explain "how I do it" when people want to know. It's like trying to explain any other natural ability—like, "How is it you sing so well?" or "How can you draw like that?" Someone with those talents might say that they practice a lot, but it's a sure bet that they were better than average at their particular ability even before they began practicing seriously. Aside from the colorful way my psychologist friend described my ability, I've often said that the job I have now is a lot like the ordinary job I held before I went public—as a receptionist, basically picking up and directing calls.

An Art, Not a Science

One difference is that the caller does not always clearly identify themselves. They might tell me their name, they may even spell it out, or they may simply give me a first initial. There can be an impressionistic aspect to it, in that I may know the name has two syllables and I'll hear part of it and the other part may be indistinct. Also, the medium is the filter through which a message is delivered, and she is limited by her own personal life experiences. So if a name is unusual, one I've never come across in my life, it can be a challenge to grasp it and I may need an assist from the client.

Receiving a message is not a perfect science; it's more of an interpretive art. I'll hear something—or more accurately, I'll get a thought in my head that runs parallel to my own thoughts; I'll see an image or smell something, like perfume or smoke or alcohol. My ability is what is called "clairsentient," which means that all my senses are psychically involved. (There are other mediums who rely more on just one of their senses. If that happens to be their sense of hearing, they would be called "clairaudient"; if they mainly are seeing visions, they would be called "clairvoyant.") I really don't know how the spirits make me smell alcohol or smoke or cologne. It just happens to me, just the same as if a living person were smoking a cigarette or wearing a particular scent. And I can always distinguish the source of the smoke, whether it's from a cigarette, a cigar, a pipe, or a marijuana joint. But the truth is I don't know if I'm actually smelling it physically using my human olfactory capabilities, or if I'm smelling it in some energetic way via my mind. It's hard to say, because it comes to me in such a way that sometimes I sense it and feel it the same way I'm smelling it. The person I'm doing a reading for doesn't smell anything, while for me it's quite clear and obvious.

Physical sensations also play a role. For instance, I've had spirits pinch me, hug me, or just use my body as an instrument to describe their own symptoms in life or the manner in which they crossed over. I may have a sensation of something very fast and dramatic, which could indicate some sort of accident. If a spirit wanted to convey that they had crossed due to a problem with their lungs, they might either visually show me this or they might create the sensation within me that would let me understand this—pain, pressure, or shortness of breath.

Over the years I've had so many different experiences with

the dead and the different ways they express themselves. They are not all the same, but by now I've got a pretty good handle on a broad range of their repertoire.

It's Not About Me

Even though they are using me to get their message through, the connection is really between the spirit and the person I'm doing a reading for. A medium is just an intermediary. I really am like the receptionist in that I first pick up a message from the spirit, I make a connection, and then I deliver the message to the intended recipient. I don't have to be near the client and I don't have to scour the universe to seek out the spirit. I can be right in front of the client or I can be across the world talking with them by phone. The spirit who is connected to that person will come to me in order to be put through to that person.

When I'm doing a reading for someone they have to help piece things together—some of what the spirit tells me may be literal, while some of it takes a bit of reading between the lines in order to give the fullest possible picture. For example, during one show I did in Totowa, New Jersey, at a Holiday Inn, this girl's father came through, but he showed himself to me as an image of Popeye the Sailor. I said, "Don't take this the wrong way, but this is what I'm seeing—he's showing me this cartoon image of Popeye." She said, "Well, he was in the navy." I said, "Was he a real character? Because he's showing me this and I get the impression he thinks he's being funny." She was laughing and she said, "Yes, that's just his personality." So with one image I got something about what he'd done in life as well as an example of his humorous nature when he was in the flesh. The fact that he had shown me this image in this way gave me a little extra so his daughter could know it was really him, because she recognized his personality as well as something specific about his life.

What people need to remember is I'm not making this stuff up. I very often don't even know what spirits are talking about. They will always try to give me something particular to the person I'm doing the reading for, something that the person will recognize even if it means nothing at all to me. I had a client named Lena whose mother had died. In the reading her mother kept showing me a cat, but it was weird because, as I told Lena, her mother didn't want me to say "cat." I said, "It's like she wants me to say 'pussy' or 'pussy cat.'" Lena confirmed that her mother was known as "Grandma Pussycat"—that was her nickname. Who knew? During that same reading I kept seeing horseshoes. I thought that was pretty strange and again had no idea what it meant. But when I asked, Lena easily solved the riddle. She said, "Concetta, hanging on the inside of all the doors in my relatives' houses are horseshoes for good luck."

Sometimes it takes guesswork on both sides. I'll never forget one show I was doing, during which this man named Dennis was taking photographs the entire time. He just seemed to me like an old soul. He was blown away when I was able to give him validation from his father. I told him that his father looked at him as a brother, not as a son. They were so close, like best friends. I also said, "There's somebody here named Holland"—an unusual name, but I knew it was a person who was telling me his name, not a reference to the country. He completely freaked out—he said, "That's my grandfather!" Then I told him, "Your father's telling me to mention Gina," and he went nuts. He went "Oh noooo! That's my ex-wife! Don't bring her up!" It was so funny—but there was more. I said, "He's trying to tell me something about dental work.

Are you having any dental work done?" He said no. I said, "Well, maybe it's something about your ex-wife?" He said, "Well, I hope it's not that I'm going to have to identify her by her dental work!" The whole audience went crazy laughing.

Sometimes the person I'm reading for may just not remember something—the experience of having a reading is not an everyday thing. A lot of people feel caught like a deer in the headlights when they have a reading. There was a perfect and very funny example of this at a recent show when I was talking to a woman and the dead guy who was coming through for her was talking about some bar where she hung out. I told her that he was mentioning the name "Michael" and asked her if she knew what he was talking about. She drew a complete blank. I said, "Who owned the bar?" She was shaking her head like not for the life of her could she make any connection with this, when the woman next to her, her sister, shook her arm and said, "Your husband!" Turned out her husband, whose name was Michael, had owned a bar, but as clear and obvious as this sounds, she literally could not connect to it without her sister practically slapping her into awareness. Of course the audience laughed when she realized, but I completely understood. For most people, it's just really strange to be talking to someone who has passed on, and the experience makes most of us a little gaga!

In a letter I received recently from a woman who attended one of my shows, I became aware of something else that can happen when people are put in this extraordinary position of hearing from a deceased loved one. What she related was that because she was so stunned by being in the spotlight, somewhat unexpectedly her perception during the reading was that not much had been conveyed. She'd witnessed numerous other readings before she was chosen to be read and had felt they were all deeper than her own. She wrote:

> But at the end of the event, I chatted with a woman and her husband. They had enjoyed my reading and felt that it was—contrary to my observation—very satisfying. We each had felt the other's reading had been more poignant than our own. As I was driving home reflecting on this new experience of hearing from my dead mother through a stranger's voice, I realized that I indeed had been like a deer caught in headlights. And perhaps this prevented me from being able to truly appreciate the value in my reading. I also realized that what you conveyed could only be as revealing and telling as the messages you receive from your dead fans. That said, let me tell you that I could barely concentrate on the other readings after my own reading. I came to your show unprepared. No paper and pen to take notes. It never occurred to me the level of focus that would be necessary for me to remember all of the messages my mother would funnel through you.

Solving a Mystery

By now, I'm sure you understand that in a reading situation the souls are providing the clues and sometimes it takes a little "Nancy Drew" to figure out what they are trying to convey. Occasionally I can inadvertently create my own "red herring"—a false clue—by projecting an incorrect interpretation onto what I'm hearing and will confuse the intended recipient of the message. I try very hard not to do this—after all, we're both attempting to solve the same mystery—but at the same time I'm also trying to get the message across. So I will make an effort to interpret and it's not always right. It's difficult to find the middle ground between not saying enough and saying too much. My ability to interpret correctly can have a lot to do with my own personal life experiences, as it does for any medium, I suppose. Once, during a reading, I was seeing a kitchen, and below the kitchen I was seeing shelves of jars with all kinds of vegetables and fruits stored in them. Well, my mother didn't cook—I was raised on Pop-Tarts. And I'm not the cook in my family—I rely on my husband, John, and my friend Mushy (a.k.a. Cornelia DiNunzio), who are both great cooks, and some wonderful local restaurants, or I'd starve. So I don't know much at all about food preparation in terms of just cooking a meal, let alone canning and preserving anything. So when I saw all this food on shelves I asked the man I was doing a reading for if his mother had a "double kitchen." That's what it looked like to me— one kitchen on top of the other. Of course, he said no. It took a lot more back-and-forth for me to describe it and for him to realize I was talking about a cellar where his mother had stored all her canned goods—the vegetables and fruits she had prepared to use later in the year.

So at times, the confusion stems from a client who can't, in that moment, recognize something that would make sense to them if they weren't in the middle of such an unusual experience. In other instances it's because I'm trying to communicate a concept or situation that I just have no experience of and I completely misinterpret it. It also can be because I'm saying a name that the soul knows, but the living client has never met or heard of the person. Perhaps it was a family member who died before my client was born, or when they were very young, or it was a friend of the deceased individual whom the client never even met. In this case, when they don't recognize someone who's mentioned I'll tell them to "just mark it down" so they can check with other family members or still-living friends of the deceased who might know what they're talking about. I can't tell you how often someone has left thinking that they didn't know someone who'd been referred to, and then on the way home it suddenly clicked for them: mystery solved! I get e-mails and letters about that all the time. But I love it if I can stay with it when they are there in front of me long enough for us all to figure it out.

As with any mystery, I often have to piece things together like a jigsaw puzzle. I might get pieces from several different parts of the puzzle but can't get them to fit until I find all the edge pieces and connect them first. When I was younger and had not been doing this for very long, I used to get frustrated when someone I was doing a reading for didn't seem to recognize what the dead person was trying to tell them. I would be embarrassed, like I wasn't doing it right, or like I thought my client would think the whole thing was fake. But after years and years of talking to dead folks, I've learned that even though they're doing their best and I'm doing my best, there can be a temporary disconnect. I really rely on my client to help piece together all the clues in order to communicate the message intended for them.

Over years of working with the dead, I've learned to keep trying, to not give up on them and move on too quickly. I remember once I was trying to describe something about a wedding and the person I was reading for didn't know what I was talking about. I heard the dead gal saying, "Stick with it, she'll get it, she'll get it!" They do know what they're talking about and usually, with a little extra effort, we can all figure it out together. Since I've learned to do this, to invest a little more effort in the unraveling and piecing together, I think I have far fewer people leaving my office or one of my big shows with the feeling that the Other Side isn't real.

At Home with the Dead

The spirits walk always among us—and for me, this is a major understatement! In my household spirits can show up pretty much anytime. I love them, but on occasion it can be like getting a call when you're just sitting down to dinner. It's not always convenient and you might be tempted to just let the machine pick up.

If I'm in my kitchen and maybe our home burglar alarm isn't turned on, and I see someone walking by out of the corner of my eye, I might initially be startled like anyone else, but I regain my composure quickly once I realize it's not an intruder. When I go to sleep, I turn on the alarm—I don't want to have to get up in the middle of the night to investigate and assure myself that the individual moving past my door in the hallway is not a live person but a spirit. But when I'm awake and the alarm is off, I'll check out every noise, whether it's a rattling noise, a knock, or anything else. One time I was in my upstairs hallway and heard bells ringing right in my ear. I have a hearing impairment, so I was wondering what the heck I heard. I walked around looking for where the sound was coming from and I went into my office, where I have a little doll no bigger than a Christmas ornament, a joker that has bells on the tip of his hat. I realized that was the noise I was hearing. The doll was on the floor. But weirdly, even though I'd been a pretty good distance away, down the hallway, it sounded like someone had taken the doll and rung it right next to my ear. I'd been with clients all day long and souls were coming and going, so it had to be a soul who had done that.

If someone needs glasses to read but they haven't got their glasses on, they're really going to have to work at seeing signs, letters, and notes, and they might not be very successful. But if they wear their glasses, they see perfectly and the words practically jump out at them. That's how it is for me with my spiritual glasses, so to speak. My glasses are always on so I'm always seeing spirits. But sometimes I just want peace; I just want to be quieter. I don't always want to see them or hear what they're trying to tell me. Fortunately, I have a relationship with them that allows me to say, "Listen, I want to watch this movie right now" (what I really say is, "In the name of God, let me be at peace now"), and they'll pretty much make themselves scarce. So it's not like I have to look for spirits in order to see them; I actually have to ask them not to present themselves in order not to see them. Let me put it another way . . . if, for example, my best friend, Mushy, has a story she wants to tell me that's really important, she'll say to me, "Let me tell you what happened at the garden club, you gotta hear this!" And I might say, "Listen, honey, right now I'm cooking dinner, I can't concentrate," or "Mushy, listen, right now I have my next-door neighbor in the house, she's dropping off a few things from her vegetable garden—I'll have to call you back." That's the same type of thing. She'll say, "Okay, I'll call you back later," or I'll say, "I'll call you back when I can talk." We hang up the phone and I go back to what I have to do, but in the back of my mind I know that Mushy is there and has something she wants to tell me. So I'll call her back, whenever I'm done taking care of whatever I'm involved in, to listen to the garden club story. The spirits are always available to me in the same way. Sometimes I'm preoccupied with other things, so I have to put them on the back burner while I'm doing my cooking on the front burner.

Whenever I do a show, I'm there—ready, willing, and able to listen to them. Or when I'm seeing a client, I'm ready, willing, and able to work with them. But other times, like when I go to sleep at night, I'm going from the Alpha to Beta to Theta to Delta states of consciousness. And those different states make it very easy for me personally to listen to the Other Side. More likely than not I'll hear messages that someone has for me or that they want me to pass on to someone else, someone I know or even a client who'll be coming to see me the next day. But sometimes I just need to sleep, so I have to say a short prayer and ask them to get back to me later!

2

Dead People and You:
Opening to a Connection with the Other Side

> "Ghost of the Future," he exclaimed, "I fear you more
> than any spectre I have seen. But as I know your purpose
> is to do me good, and as I hope to live to be another man
> from what I was, I am prepared to bear you company, and
> do it with a thankful heart. Will you not speak to me?"
> —*A Christmas Carol*, Charles Dickens

I'm convinced that everyone, to some degree, can hear and/or see spirits. The ability just may not be as developed in most as it is in someone who is naturally psychic. Think of it this way: Anyone can throw a ball, but not everyone can pitch a no-hitter. Anyone can draw a picture, but not everyone can draw a picture that might be deemed worthy of hanging in a gallery or museum. In the case of psychic ability, it's a matter of putting oneself in a particular state of consciousness and tuning in to the same frequency as the spirits. Not everyone can do it at will. Some can do it on occasion. In some cases a voice may break through into our consciousness that seems completely random and we can't repeat the experience—like taking that one perfect photograph when normally that is not your particular talent. But the Other Side is there for all of us and I believe anyone can develop their ability and form a closer relationship with the Other Side if they so desire.

Seeing Ghosts

I realize that the level of contact with the dead that I experience is way more than the average person has. But since the Other Side is literally all around us it's completely possible for anyone to see a ghost or a spirit.

Spirits can appear to you in all different forms. My friend Madeline suffers from floaters in her eyes, due to a physical condition. I personally don't have this condition, but the way she describes it is certainly similar to the way I do sometimes see a spirit—sort of a soft, intangible movement in the peripheral vision. But spirits show themselves differently, I believe, depending on our present level of consciousness. In an ordinary state of consciousness, I most often see a hazy figure that drifts by. I might see it as a shadow, or it's as if my surroundings go out of focus and I suddenly realize that there's someone there from the Other Side—a spirit, or a ghost, if you prefer—whom I'm literally looking through. Their energy is just dense enough that it creates a blurry look to whatever is just beyond them in the room. This happens frequently when I visit historical places; I see these blurry patches in the room and I know that there's an energy there wanting to communicate. This is probably the most common appearance of spirits for me—the shadowy form or the blurry patch. But I have had people tell me that they've seen a complete "physical" apparition—a full body—

and then gone on to find out that there was nobody there or it was a situation where nobody could possibly have been there. In my subconscious state I often can see them so clearly, in full detail. I've seen my mother this way, looking completely happy and healthy—just so real. This is more likely to happen when someone is in a deeper state of consciousness, not their usual alert, present-in-this-moment conscious state, but more like drifting on automatic pilot, a semiconscious state in which we do a lot of our daily tasks that are so habitual we don't have to think about them and can "space out."

I personally most often see a nearly colorless mist or haze or simply a blur when I'm looking through a soul who is present, but I've heard of others who have seen ghosts of a different color. One of my favorite stories about this is from a young man who said that while staying at his grandmother's house he saw a pinkish ghost going up the stairs. When he asked his grandmother if her home had a ghost she said, "What color was it?" Knowing full well that ghosts are either grayish or white in all their popular culture depictions, and not wanting to appear foolish, he said the ghost was white. His grandmother laughed and said, "You couldn't have seen our ghost; our ghost is pink!"

Sightings of and interactions with the dead happen more often than people realize. More and more, I see so-called "ordinary" people coming forward with their own experiences with spirits.

Dear Concetta,

I'm a 47-year-old African American female. I'm writing to you for a little help. Ever since I was a child, I was visited in the night by spirits. At about age two or three I had a near death experience, too. I drowned at the beach, following my father out into the water. I was rescued by the lifeguard and brought back to life. I believe it was soon after that I started keeping the whole family up at night seeing things and being touched by someone.

I have been having all sorts of experiences in my life. I didn't know at the time what was going on and who was communicating with me, but I just recently lost a very good friend of mine and he was the first dead person I saw clearly for a few seconds. I believe because I loved him so much. I wasn't afraid of him. I sat down in the chair I saw him in and began to talk to him. I told him I saw him and wasn't scared of him but I didn't know what was going on with me. A few seconds later I saw the vision walking away.

I attended his funeral in the Virgin Islands, St. Thomas. That night after the funeral, I was awakened early in the morning by a voice saying, I know you know, don't you? Ever since my encounter with his spirit, I do feel I have some kind of communication with him.

I do consider myself a spiritual person. I have prayed since I was a little child. I asked God to help me with this because I didn't know what was going on with me, but now I hear some of my stories—the things I've experienced—coming from other people. I have become more willing to talk about my abilities with some people.

I'm asking you to please advise me on what I should do. This is an unusual talent and people will start talking about you and calling you crazy. I'm trying my best to deal with what is happening to me all my life. Sometimes in the Black community they call it "dipping into the devil's work," as if it's something evil. I believe it's a gift and I could help others.

Thank you

I had a client who had a thirty-year-old nephew who had the mental abilities of a ten-year-old come to see me. The nephew talked to his grandparents in his room at night. This wouldn't have been unusual except that his grandparents had died. One night he told his parents that not only his grandparents were there, but also another man he didn't know. They asked him, "Who is he?" and my client's nephew described him, but his parents didn't know who this man was. Some time later they were looking at some old family photos. The nephew pointed at one of the snapshots and said, "That's the man, that's the man who I saw." The man he was pointing to, his parents knew (although they had never actually met him), was the father of the grandparents' son-in-law. They had recently heard that this man had died just two weeks before, but the son-in-law had not seen his father in thirty years.

Never Fear

The woman who wrote the letter on page 19 touched on something very important. She said she believed that she was able to see her friend because she loved him and wasn't afraid of him. Likewise, my client's nephew certainly was not afraid of his grandparents—he seemed to enjoy his conversations with them. For anyone who wishes to have the closest possible connection with a loved one on the Other Side, it's important to let the spirits know that you are not afraid to hear from them or even to see them. While many would say they'd like to hear from a deceased loved one, the majority, I think, would be startled to say the least to see one in spirit form—if not downright terrified. It's simply not an everyday experience for most people. If you do want to make a connection of this kind, you might want to try visualizing what that kind of encounter could be like, in a sense preparing yourself for the event, so if it does occur you'll be able to meet the spirit of your family member or friend with openness and love. I cannot promise you that this will bring you a spirit visitation—the spirit side has its own rules and reasons, not to mention its own timing. But by your actions you will be sending a message that they are welcome, and likely sparing yourself a heart attack in the event they do show up.

Spiritual Power Tools

There are two main tools that anyone can use if they want to have a closer connection with the Other Side: meditation and prayer. Both of these focus the energy of our minds (intentions) and hearts (desires) and send it out into the world and beyond. These tools have been absolutely invaluable to me in my life as an "ordinary human being" and in my work as a medium. While they do a professional job, they are not limited to professional use. Every day we are met with challenges, from a difficult or troubling relationship to issues with our jobs to family tragedy. We're each here for our own particular purpose (which we'll talk a lot more about later) but we are not meant to go it alone. Whether or not we have reliable help in our lives—a supportive family, a trusted friend, a mentor—we all get help from the Other Side. Our angels, our deceased loved ones, or even souls we have not met on this side but who know us and have cared for us over numerous lifetimes are watching over us and providing assistance to us through our struggles. In energetic form they work to manipulate circumstances to our benefit whenever they can—whether we ask for their help or not. But if you do need and want help from the Other Side, meditation and prayer are the best means to reach out and let them know. While closely related, the real difference between the two is that prayer is actively asking for assistance, while with meditation we may recite or chant a short prayer or mantra (a sort of spiritual word formula) to quiet and focus the mind, eliminating random thoughts that interfere with our purpose, but mainly we are in a receptive state. Instead of saying, for instance, "Please help me," or "Please be with me," or "Please protect me," we are trying to rid our minds of other things so that we might receive some helpful message or even simply calming energy when we are not at peace.

> For best results with your meditation practice, avoid using "recreational" drugs or alcohol as they can disorganize your energy, erode focus, and inhibit your ability to connect with the spirits.

Using these practices you'll find God and the Other Side are what I call AIR: Always In Reach.

What You Wear

I've been asked at times if it makes a difference what you wear—for instance, does wearing black (like at a funeral or for mourning) keep spirits away or is there some other thing that maybe attracts souls? It's a cute question. I wear things that inspire me, that make me feel good spiritually, or to put it another way, that make my spirit feel good. Things that make my spirit feel closer to God. I wear medals, I wear crosses, and I have no problem wearing the Star of David, either, even though I wasn't born Jewish. I think it's a beautiful symbol and I have one that I love to wear. But, really, do whatever turns *you* on, whatever makes *you* feel spiritually close to the energy of God—of which the souls are made (and we are as well). What you wear doesn't make a difference in the sense that if you wear a certain thing it's going to bring you the three dancing ghosts of Christmas Past, Present, and Future. There's no formula or guarantee. But if wearing a particular garment or piece of jewelry elevates your spirit, reminds you of a loved one, makes you feel spiritually closer to God—that's what's important. It's what's in your heart that matters. If wearing a certain thing when you meditate calms you or makes you feel more spiritual—if you want to hold rosary beads, for example, because it makes you feel closer to God—then use that. I get it—I do it. The reality is that we are with God wherever we are, but going to a church, a mosque, a synagogue can make us *feel* closer to God and that's why so many people go to a place of worship. So if there is something special you like to wear that brings you that feeling, by all means, use it.

Getting Through to Us

While nearly everything that the souls do for us is done anonymously, without our even realizing that we've had their help, sometimes they do want us to know that they are nearby. Because most of us are going about our days focused on what is right in front of us, we just aren't used to thinking about the spirit world, so to be honest, I don't think the spirits have an easy job getting our attention. In addition to any task or conversation we may be presently absorbed in physically, we're also usually occupied mentally, our thoughts running back and forth over things we've done and things we need to do. What options does a spirit have to get our attention?

Well, mainly, they tend to do pretty obvious things; they're not subtle. They make loud noises, turn lights off and on, maybe turn water on in the sink, knock things over, tilt pictures on an angle, sometimes send them flying through the air. On occasion they even touch us.

But each of us has another way that we most commonly get their messages, and that's our intuition. We get what we call a hunch, or we say, "I just had a feeling," or "Something just told me . . ." (that's my favorite one, because I'll say that it wasn't some *thing* that just told them, it was some *one*). Sometimes we get a feeling, like a sense of anxiety, and it can be the Other Side giving us a warning, telling us to be careful or not to do something that will result in our getting hurt or even killed. Human beings have more ability in their brains and in their souls than they ever give themselves credit for. How often have we heard someone say, "I don't know, I was in the kitchen and this horrible feeling just came over me"? Then they go on to find out that their child was in a car accident or something happened to their husband, one of their friends, or someone close to them.

When we say we're "on the same wavelength" with someone, we really are. This is literally true, spiritually, energetically. People who are close—mothers and children, husbands and wives, friends—as a matter of course use a very basic form of communication that needs no words. Say you go into a place where there's a party going on and you see a good girlfriend. Everyone is talking and laughing, munching on snacks, having a good time. But something about your friend tells you that something's wrong with her; she doesn't look right, or you got a "vibe" from her. You can just tell. How? You can't put it into words; you just know her. When I say, "you just know her," what I really mean is you're probably directing your energy toward her, reading her, or her energy is reaching out to you. But sometimes you're just not confident enough to acknowledge that, to say, "I know for sure, something happened today. What's wrong with you?"

As a medium, I can put myself into a different state of consciousness and I could know pretty certainly that something is wrong with a friend and even the nature of their trouble. But I'm a human being first, and I don't make a practice of invading a friend's space like that. I do it like everyone else. For example, the other night, four of us went out to a restaurant. We're sitting there having dinner, talking and joking, beginning to consider our orders, and I looked at my friend Charlie and said, "Something's wrong with you." He gave the usual response that people give: "No, no, I'm fine. Everything's all right." But I kept at him. I said, "Charlie, I've known you a long time. Something's wrong, what's wrong?" He said, "No, nothing, really, Concetta." I said, "Charlie, I have a feeling what it is, but I'm not sure. It's one of a couple of things—you either met somebody new and you've got this new relationship going on in your mind, or you're depressed." He said, "Well, to be honest, Concetta, this is the week that Anthony and I broke up, this is the week my mother died, this is the week that . . . ," and all these things began to pour out. He didn't want to say anything, but all I had to do was get the right key to open up Pandora's box and he let me in. I knew it was one or the other and it turned out he was depressed. If I'd allowed myself to really sit back and tune in on a deeper level I might have been able to get more information simply from his behavior, without even asking him, but I just went right to what my "ordinary" human feelings were telling me. We all have these abilities and we all do that. And it's something we can all get better at simply by making the effort. But again, with our busy lives, it's easy to become oblivious, to not focus and let ourselves feel what's going on with each other, let alone be open to hearing from the Other Side.

Visits and Warnings

Even if you feel you have no particular talent for the psychic, occasionally you still may receive a clear and direct communication. This takes a tremendous amount of effort and energy on the part of the spirit making contact with you and, though not always, it may be a message of extreme importance. This might occur when you are in a relaxed, sub- or semiconscious state, or even a dream state. For example, an elderly gentleman at one of my shows related how his father came to him "in a dream," looking young and healthy even though he had died of cancer many years before. He told me that his father did not speak, just stood before him, smiling, for a few minutes—or maybe only moments—then embraced him and disappeared. He asked me, "Concetta, was that just a dream or did my father really visit me? It seemed so real while it lasted, like it was really him." This actually is a classic example of one kind of spiritual visitation. Yes. It absolutely was really his father. People do seem to be confused or uncertain about this but it's actually very easy to distinguish between a dream and an actual visit. A dream may be long, rambling, convoluted. Scenes may change, and the dream may contain characters you don't even know even if you have the sense that they symbolize someone you do know. There is nothing symbolic in a visitation from the Other Side. The visit will usually be brief and to the point. Rarely are more than a few sentences exchanged; the spirit may speak a single word or even say absolutely nothing—all the meaning is conveyed just by their very presence: They are well, they are with you, they love you.

Even if I'm sleeping, if I see my mother and she's making sense and communicating with me, it's not a dream. I'll make a very vivid point in my consciousness to remember it. Whereas, if what I'm getting is little bits and pieces that are convoluted or don't make sense or have a symbolic quality about them, I know that this is a dream, that my mind is just playing out a theme.

Obviously we don't need to be sleeping to hear from the dead. If they need to break through they will. Again, this requires a big effort on their part, but where there's a will, there's a way. I remember another man who told me a story about how he had been driving on an unfamiliar road at night and the weather was drizzly and foggy. All of a sudden, he heard what he recognized as his father's voice in his head saying, "Stop!" Without even thinking, he slammed on the brakes, only to find out that he'd come to a stop right in front of a barricade he hadn't seen through the fog. The road was undergoing some sort of construction and there was a significant drop that he would've fallen into had he crashed unwittingly through the barricade. His father, who had crossed to the Other Side, was protecting him.

Yet another way the Other Side makes contact with us is through what we call "synchronicity," that is, arranging certain happenings or meetings in such a way that we see it as an amazing coincidence (I always say there's no such thing as coincidence), so extraordinary that it can't help but get our attention. To the ordinary person these happenstances seem beyond reason or beyond something they imagine would be "normal." They might see their mother's favorite flower on her birthday—and it might be a flower that is not even in season, or it might be in a place where there usually wouldn't be flowers, something that sets it apart. Or maybe someone who's going bowling knows their dad's bowling score and notices that the older guy in the next lane has the same first name as their dad and has the same bowling score he always had. It could be a situation where it's a league and everyone knows everyone else and this guy isn't even one of the usual players, but someone was sick and this is who was called to fill in. Someone might say, "Oh, what a coincidence," but it's really beyond what you can dismiss in this way.

I had a client who told me that when her mother died she took her mother's clothes to Goodwill. She told me that as she went through her mother's closet she had seen various pieces of clothing that prompted her to think, "I remember Mom wearing this on such and such an occasion"—there were so many things she recognized and that brought back specific memories. But she said, "You know, Concetta, I had gotten some really nice pieces of jewelry and some other things of hers, so I thought I had plenty of things to remember my mother by and I just didn't want to hang on to all these clothes even though they were loaded with memories." I certainly understand this and I do really encourage people not to hang on to too many things—it's not necessary.

To digress for a moment, I remember when my brother Harold died I hung on to nearly every single artifact he'd had in his apartment for almost ten years. It was ridiculous; I dragged this stuff around. Then after ten years I finally did get rid of it, and I honestly didn't need all that stuff to remember my brother by. But at the time I'd felt like if I got rid of it I would be getting rid of him. It's a silly way to feel, but I do understand that impulse when I see it in someone else and I sympathize. But they (the spirits) don't expect us to keep all their old stuff.

Anyway, this woman told me that among the things she took to Goodwill was a sweater. She was standing with her sister when she took the sweater out, and they were laughing about how they teased their mother one time when she was wearing the sweater, saying that she looked like the actress-comedienne Lily Tomlin doing her telephone-operator character, Ernestine—"Number, please—hello? Is this the party to whom I am speaking?"—when she was on the 1960s comedy show *Laugh-In*. They laughed and laughed because they'd always make fun of their mother when she had this sweater on and they called her Ernestine. Ernestine was a big joke among the three of them. The sweater went in the pile with all the rest of the clothes and got dropped off at Goodwill. Her mother always had tissues in the pocket of the sweater. A year later she was out shopping with her sister and they decided to get a bite to eat. They were sitting in a booth and saw a woman come in wearing the sweater. They both went, "Oh, my God, doesn't that look like Mommy's sweater?" "Yeah, it really does." The woman turned around and looked at them and they said, "We're really sorry that we're staring at you, but that sweater you're wearing just reminds us of our mother. She passed away, but she had a sweater just like that." The woman said, "Really? What happened to the sweater?" And they told her they donated it to Goodwill. The woman asked, "Where? What Goodwill?" They told her, "Rockaway, New Jersey." The woman said, "You're not going to believe it, but that's where I bought this sweater—at the Rockaway Goodwill store." The sisters said, "Really?" And she said, "Yeah, and I remember thinking that whoever had had it must be just like me because I always have tissues in my pocket and when I bought the sweater it had a tissue in the pocket." They cracked up laughing—they couldn't believe it. But the most amazing thing was, the woman gave them her name: Ernestine.

You have to admit that this is the kind of thing that goes

beyond what anyone would think of as just a coincidence. It's not just another one of those things that make people say, "I wonder if that's just something I want to believe." It was absolutely something that their mother put together and made them know. Even though these sisters didn't feel they had a special ability, they were experiencing a psychic phenomenon, that's for sure. They were experiencing their mother.

Everyone has some degree of psychic ability whether they are aware of it or not. Everyone has souls around them to help and comfort them. Everyone has a choice to believe or not believe—we can choose whether or not we want to look into our spiritual connections, experiment, educate ourselves, go farther, read books on it.

There are many more ways that an ordinary person can see the Other Side. It's just wanting to that makes the spirit world available to us. It's telling your loved ones who have passed on that it's okay for them to show themselves to you, that you're not afraid. It's looking for the simple things, not being overly dramatic in our expectations—not thinking it's going to be like Hollywood.

Be alert for synchronicities and recognize these happenings are not coincidental. Be delighted when you see these things— embrace them, believe them. Don't discount them. When you go to sleep at night pay attention to the quality of your dreams— when you are really aware, it's not difficult to discern what is a dream and what is a true visit. Trust yourself to know the difference.

It's so simple. People are always looking for more complicated instructions, way bigger signs. That's not where you should be looking. It's not impossible, but it's pretty rare that there will be some big dramatic show. However, the little signs, the tiny little things that are always happening, are around us all the time. You just need to notice.

Reminders and Practices

- Relax in the moment. Close your eyes, and count slowly from one to three. Remain quiet, be still. One, two, three—open your eyes. And remain quiet. And ask the spirits to show themselves to you, whether a particular soul or just anyone who is nearby. Ask them to make you feel calm. Invite them into your life for peace and comfort. Send them messages of love and tell them you're ready to hear something from them.

- Remember, prayer is your spiritual power tool. Tell the Other Side what you need.

3

Big God

There is nothing new under the sun.
—Ecclesiastes 1:9

Thousands of individuals who have had the experience of nearly dying only to be revived in their physical body have described making a journey toward a light of exquisite brightness and splendor, the Light of God—all-knowing, all-understanding, all-forgiving. Nearly everyone, even as they are telling their story, will say, "There are no words sufficient to describe it." They can only begin to speak of the grandeur of heaven—the light of indescribable intensity and beauty, the colors unknown to the human eye, how the heart is completely suffused with unconditional love and peace. When they return from the realm of God they know it as home and have no fear anymore of dying, even though they very often have a renewed desire to accomplish some mission before once again returning to the Other Side at the end of life.

No matter what name He is called by, no matter what religion you are, there is only one God. On the Other Side, there are no separate religions. There are not seventeen different gods on the Other Side duking it out for supremacy. The God I worship and pray to is your God. The God who protects you and comforts and provides for you is my God. God is the answer to every question and the fulfillment of every yearning and desire. When we each eventually cross to the Other Side we no longer hunger for anyone or anything; we are at perfect peace, and God is that peace.

Religion

Since it's what I did before I went public with my ability, I often use the example of a company receptionist sitting at her desk in heaven (my desk wasn't in heaven) to describe what I now do. Mr. Weisman walks in and the receptionist tells him, "Right over there, sir; the Jewish God will see you now." Here comes old Mrs. Park. "The Buddhist God is right that way. Oh, Mr. Murphy, for the Catholic God you need to go down that corridor and take a left at the end." Or, "Looking for Lakshmi and Shiva? We had to reserve the conference room for all the Hindu gods!" It simply isn't like that in heaven (also known as the Other Side). There is only one God, with no religion to divide us. The one God is a big God, and let me tell you, size matters.

People often confuse God with religion. Inasmuch as God is *all*, God is all religions, but God is also no religion. He simply is not limited in that way. Religions are a human means of expressing the awe of God, to honor and worship God, and I find it a shame that, given this, we have so much strife in the world over religion. It's so crazy! It would be like if different people were complimenting a baby, and one said how intelligent the baby looks, another noticed what beautiful eyes she has, someone else admires the baby's smile—but then, though all these observations are true, they start clobbering each other over the head because each person noticed and mentioned a *different* attribute.

I believe that every religion was founded with good intentions. And certainly every religion has something beautiful in it. Many have beautiful ceremonies as part of their worship; a local church, mosque, or temple can create a community and care for its members; many teach important spiritual lessons and encourage service and charity toward those who are needy in the world—all good and important work. When religion is able to unite us with our fellow souls it is in alignment with God and His intentions. The spiritual challenge is not to come to blows over our different perspectives of God. God does not favor one religion over another. We are intended to learn how to get along with each other and be accepting of each other in spite of these perceived differences in our perspectives.

17 June 2010
Subject: Thank You

I don't know if you actually read e-mails personally so here goes. I just wanted to let you know . . . your book actually jumped off the shelf to me at [the bookstore]. . . . I have ADHD and have a hard time focusing and concentrating, well, I have to tell you this, I couldn't put this book down. It took me only one night to read cover to cover. It was one of the most down to earth, truthful, humorous and knowledgeable books I have ever read.

I was born and raised a Roman Catholic and basically, I'm embarrassed to say, I lost my faith and stopped believing in

God and Heaven. Since reading this book, you transformed me. I contacted my Church in [deleted] to register as a parishioner and I'm looking forward to attending this Sunday's mass. It will be the first time in almost 30 years that I have stepped foot back into a church. This is what kind of an influence you have had on me and for this, I am eternally grateful. I thank you for opening my eyes and heart again. I thought this part of my life was dead. You have planted both of my feet back on the ground where they belong.

. . . I look forward to someday meeting you and if for some reason our paths don't cross, it was an absolute pleasure writing this letter to you. Thank you for changing my life.

God Bless You.

God Is *All*

Poets and spiritual leaders alike have tried to describe God, but God is indescribable other than through His creation and His works. Yet anyone who seeks Him will find Him—in nature, music, other people, love. Every day we live in the direct presence of God. How can we know that God is real? Look around you: Everyone and everything you see is God; so-called miracles are everywhere. I believe in science, but science "explains"—it doesn't create. Science has its reality and is important on this side of the veil—we need understanding to see how things work and to know the physical effects we are having on the world, and that the world is having on us, so we can be better managers and stewards of the earth. But God is the only Creator.

I know a few years ago a lot of people got into Kabbalah,

a form of Jewish mysticism. There's one thing they teach that I think speaks to this truth. That is that everything good in the world is God's Light. Kabbalists say that nothing is ever created or invented—everything already exists because God already made it all. No human being can ever create anything new that God didn't already make. We're not inventing anything, we're just discovering it, uncovering it. The only thing we can do is *reveal* God's Light (that is, any form of good). We can only clear away obstacles so that we can see the beauty that already exists. In spiritual terms, God is permitting us to unwrap a gift He has already made. In earthly terms, maybe the clouds part and reveal the sun. Or Michelangelo cuts away the stone and reveals *David*. That perfect sculpture was already within the stone—God put it there—but God gave Michelangelo the gift of being able to "unwrap" what was obscuring it so that what God had put there could be seen. Scientists do this when they say they've discovered something—in reality they just eliminated confusion so they could see clearly what is real, already created, and how it works. Anyone can do this in their own way. Not everyone can cut away stone to reveal a perfect sculpture, but we can clear away negativity and what is false in our lives to show all the real beauty that is already there because God put it there. We can eliminate false notes to find the true song. We can help remove evil to reveal the good in a situation or person. There really is nothing new under the sun. Everything true and lasting comes from God.

God Is Love

God's way is the way of peace. This doesn't just mean that we should not wage war against anyone; it also means that we want to be at peace within ourselves. At the heart of every human yearning is to have the eternal peace found in the unconditional love of God. You can take any desire you can think of and trace it back and this is what it ultimately will come to, whether we have full understanding of this or not.

On the Other Side, there's nothing but God's unconditional love; on this side, we miss that love and are forever searching for it. We all struggle here with friends, spouses, in-laws, and coworkers because we're expecting what we once knew over there in the Light of God. On this side each of us is a piece of God, struggling to get back to unconditional love. We want it so badly.

A big part of our lessons here involves learning to be better lovers—of ourselves, of each other, of this beautiful world that God created and gave us to play and learn in. So many times in my work with clients or in the readings I do at shows, a parent will come through and say, "I wish I would have been able to say 'I love you.'" Or "I tried to show it, but I know that often my child [or spouse] couldn't tell." "I always loved you, I just wasn't able to be as demonstrative as I'd have liked." We have all kinds of things working against us here. We get mad about one thing and it carries over and keeps us from letting go and expressing our love for someone even once the thing we were mad about is way in the past. Our ego just won't let us, our pride stands in our way—that kind of thing. But often when I get this type of message, the person it's intended for will say, "Yes, I did know. I always knew he really loved me but just couldn't show it. But I'm trying to do better. I'm trying to be a different person than my dad was. I'm trying to tell my kids and my wife every day how much they mean to me." So we do evolve. And sometimes even a negative example can really lead to a positive change because a decision is made on this side not to repeat what didn't work very well before, what they saw as a problem in someone else. I love delivering this kind of message, though, because even if the person here really did know that their parent cared about them in spite of every appearance, it's so healing for them to actually hear the words.

God has given each and every one of us gifts; He has given us all we need to love and be loved, to be happy and succeed both in spiritual terms and in earthly terms. We might resist believing this because on this side of the veil everything we do meets opposition. Expressing our love can be scary; using our gifts and getting to that happiness can require tough decisions and actions from us. In heaven, we have complete fulfillment, but here we need to work with the constraints of the physical world. We have things to push against and overcome. But we can do or be anything that is within our nature, and our guardian angels, as emissaries of God, will be there to help us with our endeavors. All of this we'll discuss in the chapters ahead.

God's Love at First Sight

I just want to stick with the subject of love for a moment. The phenomenon we call "love at first sight" is a real thing. Even if it's never happened to you, you probably know someone who was out somewhere, looked across the room or maybe was just being introduced to someone, their eyes met, and they just knew that they had each met their soul mate—or if not their soul mate, at least someone with whom they had a deep connection, who would play a starring role in their life for a time. The experience is nothing short of electric—it gets our full attention—and whenever this occurs you may be sure that it's someone, or some *ones*, from the Other Side who is arranging the timing and doing the steering to be sure that this meeting will occur. We can never know the time or place but if love is what you are looking for, just know that you've got angels working overtime to try to bring it to you. But what I want to talk about here is a different kind of "love at first sight."

Not long ago I found myself in a particularly bad mood. I'd had one of those mornings when things just seem difficult and it was a few days before I was going to be taping a TV segment with the Learning Annex that would be sent out internationally via satellite. For a week or more I'd had a sinus infection and I kept hoping it would get better before I had to go in front of the cameras. I was walking around the mall and my nose was running and I was thinking, "Damn! I can't believe I've got this stupid sinus infection. Why did I have to have it now when I want to look good on TV?" A little clique of teenage girls smacked into me, paying no attention, like I wasn't even there, and I was just getting ready to give them a piece of my mind when my eye fell on a middle-aged woman coming toward me, pushing a young girl in a wheelchair. It was clear something was seriously wrong with the girl; she was visibly disabled, with her arms and hands drawn up in atrophy and her face contorted, perhaps with muscle spasms.

This was the reality these two shared, one who had problems so significant that she was not likely to have any kind of ordinary life, and the other whose role was caring for her—a burden I can only imagine to be incredibly tough, even when there is deep love and understanding. I passed by these two in just a brief instant, really seconds, but just that quickly I literally experienced love at first sight, just as if it were an electric current zigzagging between the woman, the young girl, and me. That quickly I understood how blessed I really am. I felt complete, unconditional love.

I immediately said a silent prayer: "Thank you, Lord, for the gifts you've given me, and thank you so much for the love you've sent here in this girl who will touch so many lives and give us the opportunity to gain awareness, change and grow." This girl made such a sacrifice for all of us here who would encounter her and have the chance—simply by comparison—to know and appreciate how blessed we really are.

Often we feel uncomfortable when we see someone like this because without doing anything they make us realize how self-centered we are and how forgetful we are of what we have. They are not here to judge us, but to let us reflect on ourselves and understand how great our blessings are. It's amazing how powerful this is. One minute I was mentally bitching about my sinuses and the next my entire attitude had changed. What did it matter if I had to blow my nose in front of millions of viewers? Who cared? It had seemed important only moments before and then suddenly it was just as clear that it really wasn't important at all. All the negativity I'd been carrying with me throughout the day just disappeared. Everything was back in perspective—all the little annoyances were so unimportant. I was filled with love and gratitude for this pair who exemplified and exuded pure love, gratitude for the truly blessed and abundant life I lead and gratitude for God and His angels, who'd arranged for these two to cross my path and heal me in that moment. Just one second, just one look, was all it took for my entire attitude and outlook to change. Truly, love at first sight.

It's not only other people that can give us that transformative love-at-first-sight feeling. God has created for us such a miraculous world. Even in the midst of a deep sorrow, wild nature has the ability to buoy us up or take our breath away and heal us with its splendor. So can a lovely, peaceful garden—the co-creation of God and a loving human being with artistry and a green thumb. The animals and birds God has created and surrounded us with have the power, just by their very existence, to soothe and cheer us, as do the arts—music, dance, painting, movies, and storytelling.

Feelings are fleeting on this plane. We can't just "find" love and expect that all our problems will be forever solved. It's up to each of us every day to re-create, reenact moment-to-moment, love. On the Other Side love is the constant state, the air we breathe.

The Drama of Heaven and Earth

Oftentimes a client will tell me that their child has said something about what it was like when they were in heaven, before they were born. They remember who was there with them—frequently someone my client knows, a family member who has crossed in his or her lifetime. They may mention a choice they were allowed to make before coming here, like they were sitting on God's knee discussing the matter. This is not quite the case. On the Other Side, it's not like we are "hanging out" with God, like God is a separate being and we are gathered around Him or sitting in His lap. No. We actually merge with the energy of God; we become one with God. Here we are also of God and contain His spirit, but it is less apparent to us; the body creates an illusion of separateness. This is difficult for me to describe as I'm still on this side, but I believe on the Other Side we are aware of God and feel Him with a deeper consciousness.

We come to earth to learn lessons, make corrections for things we've done wrong, and become ever more aligned to God's ways. We'll experience comic episodes as well as tragedy. All will laugh and all will grieve. We may play many roles in a single lifetime, and the child who was able to tell her mother about the plans she made with God may forget all about that by the time she's in first or second grade. Likely when she's handed her script, so to speak, for this lifetime, she'll look at it like she's never seen it before. She'll have no clue what other actors have been cast to play in this "movie" with her. But God is present in every scene. We are surrounded on all sides by guardian angels, spiritual aides, our loved ones who have crossed before us to the Other Side, and even souls we may never have known who are connected to us in some caring way. All of these souls and spirits are working with us, for us, to guide and protect us and act as directors, producers, and stagehands in this big drama we call life.

A woman who came for a reading once told me a story about when she was in Catholic school. There was a particular priest who always looked at her with an expression she never could understand. But as she described it, he appeared to know her. Or like he wanted to say something to her but never could. She told me that she'd never really had an understanding of the whole Catholic school thing. She felt no connection to speak of with God and didn't consider herself religious. But after she had graduated and left the school, she was sleeping one night and in a "dream" (which I would actually call a "visit" rather than a "dream") this priest came to her and said, "Please pray for me." She was puzzled by the dream because, as she said, she didn't really feel like she knew the priest in any special way, and she hadn't seen him since she'd left the school. But later she found out that this priest had stopped to help someone stranded on the roadside and he was murdered. She wanted to understand the unspoken connection she shared with a man she never really knew. The priest came to her in the reading, thanking her for the prayers, and he told her he loved her. I believe that this was a way for God to bring something together for both of them, give them both some peace. There are numerous possibilities for exactly what this encounter meant. She'd had little understanding of the Other Side. Now she told me she felt she had her very own guardian angel, one she knew and believed once loved her in another time. All of it came together for her in one brief moment. I felt that he knew her from another lifetime. He felt love for her while he was here and did not know how to express it. She felt closer to God knowing this soul loved her and had come to her in the reading.

Over here, we are the actors. We have roles to play. We do have our free will—or we could call it "artistic license"—but we are not calling the shots and angles. We're not the casting agents. Usually only in limited ways do we get to decide who else is in the movie or who will play with us.

Our Connection with the Other Side

On this side of the veil there is so much chaos, confusion, and illusion. We may have every good intention, but even so, it's easy for us to lose our way. Some are so completely lost that it's not until their physical death brings them back to the Other Side to regroup, heal, and prepare for a next go that they ever recover themselves. There are many forces at work to bring us back into alignment with God—I'm far from the only one doing this work. But as a medium I like to think that through my work I can sometimes help a soul here remember their purpose and get back on track.

I had a girl who came to see me recently; she had been a somewhat regular client but I hadn't seen her in three years. She told me that the first time she had come for a reading she was an alcoholic. Her father, who had also been an alcoholic, had died when she was only three years old and she considers this event to have affected everything in her life, making her very angry and bitter. She did not believe in any God or an afterlife or anything. But, she said, the messages I'd given her were so accurate, and what I'd told her had been so inspirational, that she now had a belief in God and she had been sober and a recovering alcoholic for the past three years. I was certainly very proud of her that she had not had a drink in three years, but I was most proud of the fact that she now believes in God. I loved that she said the reading had given her that inspiration. I was quick to tell her that it was her father, through the reading (and in reality it was God speaking through her father), who had given her that inspiration, not me.

When we come to this side, our soul carries a small particle of God embedded within. This connects us to the Other Side when we are here, allowing us to be in touch with our guardian angels, or more accurately for most of us, allowing our angels to be in touch with us. It's this "God particle," if you will, that acts like an internal GPS, guiding us, helping us keep to our life's purpose—even when we are not aware of it—so long as it is not overridden by that other gift from God: our free will.

I'm always saying that heaven is perfection; we're in the tough spot here, the vale of tears, and it really is our tears that make us human, that connect us all. Over here we have imperfect understanding. There's a lot of distortion. When the spirits speak about God, the most common thing they tell me is that He is all-forgiving, all-loving. When we die it is like going home after a long trip. We are met by a loved one with open arms, as if they were welcoming us in with a hot meal and warm bed to sleep in. Someone who loves us and wants to hear all about our trip.

Angels tell me of the great spirit of God, the divine love of God. I hear it and see it everywhere. God is a perfect state of love. Perfect love asks for nothing, and it needs nothing. God needs nothing and does not ask for anything. Realize that God accepts us as we are, for who we are, but we're still here to learn to become one with God. The goodness of God is in every one of us; we have to make the choice to know Him and believe in His will. Then we shall see God. We are all sent here to live as God would have us live; that is our challenge. We're all struggling to do that.

Reminders and Practices

- When you wake in the morning, say a prayer. Ask God to be with you throughout the day and to help you with your work. Ask God to bring you peace, to ease your worries and concerns, to soothe your sorrows, calm your mind.

- Look for love at first sight and let yourself be suffused with gratitude for the sacrifice another soul has made to remind you of all you are and have.

Energy and the Body

Good for the body is the work of the body, good for the soul the work of the soul, and good for either the work of the other.

—Henry David Thoreau

Your birthday suit suits *you*—you'll never find a better fit.

—Concetta Bertoldi

Why is it that if we really are souls we come here in a body?

It's such an age-old question and it speaks to the very heart of the relationship between the spiritual plane and the physical plane. The answer is that nothing that is not challenged can change. We need the physical reality of separateness in order to have something to rub up against, something external to ourselves that does not permit us simply to exist as we are—without the grain of sand irritating it, the oyster would produce no pearl. Without being rubbed, gold doesn't shine. So basically we're here to be irritated, buffeted, and buffed, for all the right reasons.

The body is for locomotion—to get us from place to place, in an intentionally limited way (effort required!). The body is for experiencing pleasure. The body is the means and sometimes the medium of the soul's self-expression. The body enables us to experience connection with one another. The body enables us to experience creation. The body—its various parts, appendages, and organs, along with the six senses that we experience through the body (sight, sound, touch, taste, hearing, and intuition)—is God's gift to us and our best teacher here on earth. You can't really separate the human body your soul resides in from the rest of the physical experience, because it *is* your physical reality. Your appearance, your state of health, and how you process your perceptions (the information you take in through each of your senses) all affect your experience.

Now and again you'll hear someone say, "My body is a temple." That's nice—I agree that as a gift from God, our bodies are sacred like a temple. But I think beyond that it's a little hard to understand exactly what that means. I really love what the nature lover and poet Henry David Thoreau said in the quote that opens this chapter. I think it perfectly describes the relationship between our soul, our spiritual nature, and the body of flesh we wear. The soul is not constrained by the body—it roams freely when we are in a dream state and it reaches energetically beyond the body when we use our intuition. But even when we use our intuition, it works *with* the body and *through* the body. The information the soul gathers registers in the body as, for example, a "tickle" in the brain (making a connection or recalling something or someone), a tingle at the back of our neck (sensing someone is behind us or watching us), a warm feeling at our core (telling us we can trust someone), or a funny or uncomfortable feeling in the gut (telling us to be careful). The work we do using our body and the experiences we have in physical form affect our soul—to its betterment, hopefully—and the spiritual work we do may be reflected in the body in a higher state of general wellness. Of course not every use we put our bodies to will be positive. We can learn from our misadventures as well as our good deeds. But even what we learn in negative endeavors is intended to result in our making a correction (sometimes called "character building").

What many don't realize is that the soul and the body both are energy. On the Other Side, in spirit form, we have a perfected "body" of purified energy, whereas on this side, in physical form, we are composed of a much denser, heavier energy. The two forms of energy might be compared to the difference between someone walking through a room carrying an armload of roses versus a skunk walking through the room. Each leaves a lingering aroma, but the rose scent will be light, uplifting, while the scent left by the skunk will be heavy.

"Energy" comes from a Greek word meaning "activity, operation" and it literally is what keeps everything in motion; it is the animating force. Energy may be transferred or may change form, but it can never be destroyed. Every single thing that exists is made up of energy.

Everything we do requires energy, as does everything we say—it takes energy to form words and push them out through our vocal cords so they can be heard and understood. Our actions require energy and they transfer energy; you are giving your energy to a particular action, devoting your energy to a particular cause that you care about—we hear these expressions every day but don't consider how literally they can be taken. It requires that we use our energy when we speak, and our words *carry* energy. Depending on our intention and our execution, our words and actions can carry and transfer positive energy or negative energy, and the energy we move can be very weak or it can have a lot of force.

On this side we experience energy in three basic forms: electromagnetic, which is the type of energy responsible for attraction; kinetic, the energy of motion; and thermal, which produces heat and light. Each of these has particular functions in the way things work, but we usually don't think about which we are using at a given time. We can get up out of a chair and walk across the room without saying to ourselves, "I better get my kinetic energy going." Or a healer might rub her palms together before placing them on someone's injury without contemplating that she is accessing her thermal energy. We simply employ—and deploy—our energy pretty much subconsciously. That said, when we wish to use energy to exercise our free will, to turn our dreams into reality, it must be focused.

A lot of people will say that it's all about the intention, but that isn't true. There are many things we may intend but if we don't *focus* on that intention and bring enough energy to it, it will remain weak and we may never carry it out at all, or we may do it with only half the effort really required and it'll be done badly. So the execution is as important as the intention. It's about follow-through, focusing enough of our energy to make our best intentions our accomplishments. This is why the adages "The road to hell is paved with good intentions" and "We are known by our actions" are both true. The first means that we may have the best intentions in the world but if we don't follow through on them the result could be the opposite of the heavenly perfection we say we want. The second says that what we do follow through on is how people will come to know us, for better or for worse, but if our intentions are good and our follow-through is good, the result has a very good chance of being good. So, we *are* energy and we express ourselves, who we are, the kind of person we want to be, through the ways we *use* our energy. Exchanges of energy are responsible for every effect we see, initiate, or experience.

Transferring Energy

Every day, with every interaction, we are transferring energy. It's necessary for us to have this give-and-take (which we can get through animals as well as from other human beings) or our energy becomes depleted and we lose vitality—you often see this in a person who just keeps to himself and has no interaction with others. They just seem like the lights are out in the house, like they are always a little sad, depressed. When I do my workshops one of my favorite parts is introducing everyone to the art of hugging. This might sound strange since everyone assumes that hugging is old hat, that it's not something you need to be taught. But here's what we do. I'll randomly pair everybody up with someone they don't know and then ask them to give each other a hug. It's pretty funny. So many of them seem completely stiff and give their partner a stilted little arm's-length clutch. Maybe they giggle, a little embarrassed, and then they back off and look over to me, like, "Okay, we did it. Can we move on?" Oh, come on! We can do a whole lot better than that. I'll pick another volunteer—or maybe even someone who is a bit reluctant—and give them the full-body bear hug. Why? Because here's the secret: When we hug someone we give them our energy, but we are also getting energy back.

Human beings need hugs. Whether they think they want them or not—it makes no difference. And when you give them a hug, they can't help energetically expressing a deep gratitude that is literally like they are putting a power pack of energy right into your pocket. They may be completely unaware, because it happens at an unconscious level with most people. When I hug someone, I know that I'm giving them very special loving energy that is deeply healing. But I'm also aware that I'm getting this wonderful energy back from them. So when I give a hug, I don't treat the person like they might give me the swine flu, or maybe cooties. I hug like there are no walls between us and let the loving, healing, happiness-producing energy flow.

Our guardian spirits on the Other Side know when we are missing the healing energy of touch and often will come to us and bring us a shot. I had a young girl come to me wanting to hear from her father. When I connected with his spirit he reminded her that she'd had a dream of him recently, but that it wasn't really a dream, he'd literally visited her. He told her that he knew she'd felt him touching her. This validation was very dear to her because she said her father had loved to dance but he'd been bedridden for years before he died. It broke her heart. He couldn't dance or even walk. But in this dream he had come to her and they'd danced together and she could feel her hand in his hand and his other hand on her back. The feeling was so real to her. Then he took her back to her bed and said, "Okay, darling, I have to go back to Mommy now." And then he left. She woke up right away but said that she could still feel her hand in his and his hand on her back.

Although this gentleman chose to appear to his daughter in a physical shape, obviously, being pure energy, spirits don't need a body in order to transfer energy to us. You can think of it in terms of cyberspace and fiber optics and satellites for our phones and our televisions. They're out there even if we can't see the channel and how it connects to this side. The technology is mostly invisible. But we're getting our phone messages, our e-mail, we're sending photos from our phone, we're getting our TV shows. You can't see it as it's happening. But energy is being transmitted through space to make our communications systems work on this side of the veil. Well, on the Other Side of the veil, they're energy, too. They're making things happen on this side. All they have to do is focus on it. Another example would be an electric cord plugged in the socket—it's not the cord that makes an appliance work. It's the invisible energy running through the cord that makes it work. With the human body, we might think, for instance, that the muscle moves the arm. It's really not the muscle that moves the arm—it's the thought in the brain (or mind) that sends a message via the nervous system telling the muscle to move. It begins with a thought. The thought directs the energy. Spirit does the same thing. It focuses and sends a message in energy form.

Even though energy can be directed, both by us in our physical form and by spirits, it truly has no beginning and no end. This is a very difficult thing to explain and with my limited (make that nonexistent) education on the subject I can't explain it technically or in detail; I can only trace the edges with the examples I've given. Even though I've used the example of technology, in some ways I feel like primitive humans were more aware of this. We lost our conscious connection with this when we began handing over the spiritual reins to science. Many indigenous peoples worked with energy and spirit. American Indians even did what they called "shape-shifting," changing form energetically, just as the Other Side works with energy to manifest certain things here.

For example, if a spirit wanted to send a message to someone here they might show that person a particular type of bird or butterfly or other animal that would be meaningful to that person. I'm not sure if in such a case they are actually shape-shifting—if they are manifesting energetically into a butterfly—or if they are just able to energetically direct the butterfly to someone. I do believe that the energy form that spirits are in can manifest as many things, maybe anything of their choice. Remember that whatever they are doing, it's to get a message to you, and (with rare exceptions I'll discuss in chapter 10) it's always based on love and protection.

Needless to say, the process is invisible. If a spirit wants to move a book, its directed energy can do it. We don't see someone stand there and pick up the book and throw it, but again, with all our technology, it's not the wires that we see that make something work, it's the energy running through the wires. Similarly, we don't (usually) see a spirit in energy form. But they are all around us in the next dimension—they are there next to us at all times.

Emotions, Feelings

Our emotions are where the spiritual meets the physical. In terms of our six senses they are closely related to our intuition because they are about feelings. But if you look at the word "emotion" you'll notice it contains the word "motion," so it's also about movement—our feelings move us. Primarily we are here to feel life, all its expressions and possibilities—does it feel good, does it feel bad?—and be moved by this. We're here to make choices based on what we feel. On the Other Side we're in a perfect state of harmony, peace, and bliss. Here, our emotions may change in a fraction of a second. We may experience a calm emotional state, but we might also experience turmoil—anger, fear, uncertainty, anxiety. It's like our "interior weather." We look at the sky (or we look inside) and notice that it's clear and sunny, or it's stormy, or it's been dry so long that it really *needs* to rain! When we make choices about our behavior based on what we are feeling emotionally, what we're really trying to do is take our negative emotions and bring them back into a balanced state of peace, back to clear, blue skies. From split-second changes in our emotions we learn about our values—what makes us feel comfortable or uncomfortable emotionally. On the Other Side, we don't need to even consider this because we're in a perfect state, in tune with God, with perfect love.

Multiple Lives and the Body

Another aspect of the relationship between soul and body comes from our past lives. We may have certain anxieties that seem to have no root in this life—these can be especially hard to deal with because we don't know clearly where they are coming from. They may be patterns "worn in the carpet" from many lives walking the same path without being able to make a change. Or we may have particular bodily strengths or weaknesses that likewise seem unexplainable. The soul carries past-life wounds and lessons and these will be deposited accordingly throughout the body we are in today. We all go through different experiences in an individual lifetime, but over many lifetimes, we go through many, many different things. I really think that's why many people have certain fears and phobias they can't explain—they didn't come from this lifetime. The last time we were here, whatever we went through, the memories are all carried in our soul. Every day is another opportunity to experience things, and to record our experiences of the positive and the negative, and it's another opportunity to challenge ourselves to change negative behaviors, balance negative emotions, and bring ourselves more into alignment with peace, with God.

Hard to believe, perhaps, but we choose whatever body we're born in. Whatever lessons are attached to it are known to God and probably known to us at the soul level, but at the moment we're not realizing it. We agree to come here in a body that isn't perfect—*no* body is perfect—because in the core of our soul we know that it is perfect for our mission here and also that when we cross back to the Other Side we will again be in a form of perfection. We agree to come here in whatever state we are in for the purpose of learning various lessons. Like a fireman who hangs up his coat or a policeman or a soldier who hangs up his uniform, we're going to hang this body up after we complete the job and go back to a perfect form. But all the experiences are stored, like smoke in the fireman's coat.

Sometimes we agree to come here under circumstances that are really crummy. I know that we make a decision with God about the situation we'll be in before we come here. That may sound totally crazy—it sounds that way even to me. I know you really have to ask yourself, why would someone come here knowing they're going to die in a tsunami? Why does someone come here knowing they'll die at twenty years old? Why would someone agree to come here knowing they're going to have some horrible physical condition? I don't know the answer to these questions—the answer will be individual to each soul, even if they are involved in something with many other souls. I just know that we definitely make this decision.

Empathy and Compassion

The human body allows us to have an infinite array of experiences, to feel every emotional state, and to make corrections of spirit and grow ever closer to God. We have to come here to learn because on the Other Side of the veil, it's perfect. There are no lessons there—all the whys of a particular life are answered on the Other Side. On this side we have experiences that hopefully bring knowledge. On the Other Side our knowledge becomes understanding, wisdom. The big overall lesson we learn through multiple lives in different physical forms is compassion.

We can't learn compassion by osmosis.

I suppose it's almost like someone said to you, "I got a flat tire, and I had to change the tire," and you said, "Oh, really? You had to change the tire?" "Yeah." "Well, what did you do?" "Well, I had to go to the trunk, get a jack out, make sure the spare tire wasn't flat, too. Had to drag it out of the car, put it on the ground, find a way to work the jack. Then I had to get the lug nuts off, then I had to jack up the car to get the tire off, put the new tire on, put the lug nuts on, screw them on tight, put the hubcap back on." If we try to explain a situation to somebody who hasn't personally experienced it, they really won't completely understand. Maybe someone says to you, "You know what, I just lost a baby. I carried her for nine months and the baby died." Maybe they say, "I just went through a divorce; my husband left me after forty years of marriage." You have a listening ear to this person, and you think you have compassion. You think you have empathy and you can understand and be soothing to that person. But truth be told, only after you've changed the tire on that car yourself, felt the lug nuts in your hand and dragged the tire off the car and learned how it feels to be in the position of being on the road without assistance, can you really understand how it felt and truly be empathetic. It's the same thing with losing a baby or having a husband leave you; you won't truly understand how it feels unless you've experienced it yourself. I believe that all of us have come back many times to this side of the veil and that we have plundered, raped, killed— and have also been the victim of the plunderer, rapist, killer. We have gone through so many different experiences here on this side of the veil and have learned from each one of them. And I also believe that these experiences in the body teach our soul compassion. We as human beings have layers of all sorts of things in our soul. And at the very bottom are blessings—always there and always available to us. At the very bottom is God. But it's a process of refinement. Until we learn how to get rid of the crap that's on top of them, it's hard to get to the blessings. So what we're here doing is learning how to get rid of the crap so we can get to the blessings. All these experiences we go through connect us to our soul and being one with God. So the body experiences all these different things; it's necessary for us to know what it really feels like—not to just "know it" from the Other Side.

Evolution

We have much more ability than we ever can imagine contained in the physical body. Someday I know we're going to evolve to the point where we can cure ourselves from every ailment—some are already doing this—or communicate across long distances without phones. Think about it! Look at how far we've come with our technology. Did you ever think you'd be able to walk around, pick a phone out of your pocketbook, talk into it without even dialing, ask for information, and have the information just appear on a screen about twice the size of the face of your watch? That's how far we've come since Alexander Graham Bell first got the idea for telecommunications; just imagine what will happen when we begin to more seriously explore our own energy in the human body. It's just a question of dreaming, visualizing, and embracing it, exercising it and making it happen.

This is how all our technological miracles have happened. The way of the spiritual realm is imagine it, and it is. On the physical plane more effort is required. But we first need to imagine something before we can realize it. It's easier to see this with advances outside ourselves, like technology; we just need to recognize that it's the same principle with our own human capabilities. We can do the same thing with our own energy, our own souls, our own bodies. Eventually we will be able to communicate telepathically, like aliens in a sci-fi movie. Once we can visualize it, we get our minds around it and get a level of comfort and acceptance about it, and pretty soon it really is that way. (Right now I'm still waiting for a few things, like those little gadgets they had on *Star Trek* that make you all sparkly and beam you out of your living room and into the mall without having to find a parking space.)

So we're setting the bar for ourselves. We actually, I believe, could do many of these things that we still think we can't now— cure ourselves or have direct communication, person-to-person, from one side of the world to the other. We're just so preoccupied with all the stuff we're taking care of in our lives, with our responsibilities, what we want, and what we don't want, that we don't make the time to stop and think of what our possibilities are.

Here on earth, one of our biggest blessings is our ability to experience living in a physical body. In fact, many who have crossed over and are living in spiritual perfection are still eager for another chance to experience a physical human form. While this is a double-edged sword—we all experience aches and pains, some have debilitating or very limiting physical conditions, and most of us will physically decline before we cross to the Other Side—our bodies are the source of many of our greatest material-world pleasures. From the simple pleasure of lying in soft grass on a warm summer day to human physical intimacy or the unconditional love given and received by stroking a pet, these are the joys of our physical form.

Reminders and Practices

- Use all of your six senses: Lie in the grass and experience how it feels, the soft and the sharp, the solidity of the earth beneath you. Smell the scents that surround you. Look up to see the branches and leaves swirling and swaying above you against the sky. Listen to the sounds around you—do you hear birds, children playing? Try the same thing beside a lake or on the beach—reach out and let the sand sift through your fingers; listen for cheerful shouts, radios playing, the crash and rush of waves and water. Breathe deeply—salt and suntan lotion. Peel an orange, appreciate the tangy scent, and taste its mix of sweet and tart.

- Hold a loved one in your mind and energetically send them love, or send someone who is ill your own healing energy.

- Thank your body for the miraculous gift that it is—treat it to a massage!

- Pet an animal, hug a friend.

5

Soul Contracts and Life Lessons

I could well imagine that I might have lived in former centuries . . . my life as I lived it seemed to me like a story
that has no beginning and no end.

—Carl Jung

A few weeks ago, a woman came to see me and told me about
her daughter, who was seven years old. She said, "It was the most
amazing thing. A relative came to visit and we were sitting at the
kitchen table looking at some photos she'd brought with her. I've
never had a lot of family photos and I've moved a lot, so somehow
even those I did have, many of them have disappeared over time.
In any case, my daughter picked out one photo that happened
to be of her grandfather who had died before she was born. She
said, 'Oh! It's James!' I was really shocked. I said, 'You know him?'
She said, 'Yes, I knew him before I even knew you. When I came
here he sent me down in an elevator.'" I've heard countless similar
stories, so for me maybe the most extraordinary part of this one

is that her daughter was so old. Most of us, by the age of seven, have completely forgotten all we ever knew about the Other Side. And as we get older, we have very few memories of things that happened to us before the age of, say, eight, other than stories we've been told or things we've seen family photos of. The fact that this woman's daughter had never met her grandfather, had never seen these photos before, had recognized him immediately and called him by his right name convinces me that this was a genuine memory of a time before coming here, when she was on the Other Side.

Nearly every spiritual tradition in the world operates with some belief in reincarnation, the idea that our physical body may die, but the soul goes on and returns again to earth at some time in a different physical body. We've all been here before and nearly all of us will be here again. Most of us just don't remember the other times we've lived. We don't remember being on the Other Side in between lives, and we rarely remember, on this side of the veil, the agreements we made for our lives here. So I understand that people could question whether this is true or not.

I look at it this way: How many people can remember the things they've done just in this life? Hardly anyone remembers being born, and few remember the first several years of their life. Most of us can't remember the details of what we did last week, although some highlights probably stand out—like maybe we had a dentist appointment or met a friend for lunch, or had a big project due at our job. But a year from now will we even remember those highlights? A year from now they won't even seem like highlights (unless the friend dropped a bombshell of some kind during lunch)—they'll just be lost to time. My point is, if we can barely remember the details of this lifetime, we shouldn't expect to recall other lives in other bodies, other times, and other places as if they happened only yesterday.

Why Do We Return?

Most spiritual teachers would agree that we come back to this side of the veil over and over in order to balance our karma, to learn lessons of love, faith, empathy, and kindness, and to become more like God, more one with God. How we do that will be entirely individual and for each lifetime our objectives are basically threefold:

1. General refinement/purification—This means making day-to-day choices that are positive, learning—sometimes by trial and error—right from wrong, what works, what doesn't, what hurts and what helps. Over time, this behavior hopefully becomes second nature to us, but this doesn't mean we won't still hit the occasional challenge or be tempted to choose the wrong thing. Included in this category might be learning to handle our relationships with integrity, doing our part of any work, not taking more than our share of something, not taking something that doesn't belong to us, helping others when we can— basically just being a good and decent person.

2. Learning lessons/teaching lessons—Each life has some larger "projects," if you will, particular things we need to work on that we've either messed up in the past or simply have had no previous experience with. We may be put in a difficult position, a hard life circumstance, that we need to handle with grace or that may even require courage. This

could involve dealing with a physical handicap or being in a group or class that is looked down on or mistreated by a dominant culture. It could be dealing with poverty, some form of addiction, or single parenthood. It could also be simply being born into the opposite gender of the one your soul has been most often identified with in past lives.

3. Accomplishing a particular purpose—This is more a "mission" that we need to fulfill. It may have to do with bringing others together or being a catalyst for something to happen. It may involve making a discovery or changing a way of looking at something that will advance both life on the physical plane and souls on the spiritual plane. It could involve working with others or be a challenge that you alone will face. It may require a great sacrifice. Not everyone who returns, though, will have a particular mission in each lifetime—I'll talk more about this in the next chapter.

In each of these, our karma is involved, and to do all this we need to find our own unique path. Our path is made up of our interests, our beliefs, work we are drawn to, places and people we are drawn to—in other words, the fabric that comprises our life and against which our lives play out. We'll get to this in a moment.

The Soul Contract
Each time we complete a life and return to the Other Side we receive a life review. We go over what we did well and what we could have done better, and consider what we want to improve when we return. If we've made what we now see as a big mistake (maybe

treated someone badly or simply wasted a big opportunity), we might be in line for a "karmic correction," that is, a challenge that is geared toward remedying or atoning for this error. Even if we don't have anything so egregious to make up for, before we return to the physical plane we still have to make a choice and agree on what this new life will be about, what we hope to accomplish, what challenges we'll take on. We decide with God which family we'll be born into and our physical condition. Everything is for a reason. Think of it as a "Soul Contract." From what I understand about the Other Side, God doesn't just give us marching orders and ship us back to the planet. There may be a strong suggestion, but we can choose to accept a mission or not. When we are on the Other Side in spirit form we know intuitively what we need to do to take ourselves to the next level of purification and spiritual alignment. God helps us to decide, but we always have a choice. I do believe we choose, with God, what is best for everyone. We're involved with a lot of souls both there and here. There's a lot of interdependence involved in our missions.

All that said, a Soul Contract is not written in stone—we don't have one preordained "fate" that will happen to us no matter what we do. We have free will. As circumstances arise we can change our mind, alter our course. In other words, we have the ability to renegotiate our contract.

Finding Your Path
Returning to the physical plane is accepting a challenge, but what makes it even more difficult is that we quickly forget our reasons for coming back. We forget everything we knew by the time we need to use it. When we are babies or toddlers we still may have fairly direct access to the Other Side. (It's more common than

most realize for the very young to see and communicate with guardian angels—our deceased loved ones.) But as we begin to identify more strongly with this plane, most of us lose that ability and most of us forget what we knew before we got here, including what it was we came here to do. By the time we're teens we might be sitting there thinking that our parents don't get us (Did I *really* pick these parents?) and we don't like the way we look (*No way* I chose this body!). The high school guidance counselor's asking us, "What do you want to do with your life?" and we're thinking, "How on earth did I get here? And what do I do now?"

Yes, there are those seemingly lucky ones who apparently have it all figured out (and I say "apparently" because so many things can change in a lifetime and even those who start out with single-minded focus may wander at some point onto a different path). And many have parents who want to urge them in one direction or another. But many are just lost. Sometimes it takes our gaining some maturity, finding our footing in the world at large, before we can discover our path. Sometimes we simply have to be patient until our path finds us.

One way to gather clues about our true path is simply to look at the natural abilities and talents we have. These are all gifts from God but they are not handed out equally or indiscriminately. Each person gets what they uniquely are intended to get—tools that God knows that person will need in this lifetime as well as certain gifts that may simply enhance our enjoyment here. If we have one strong talent it can be a no-brainer to be led by that and see where it takes us. It's almost more difficult to have many gifts and abilities because it can take time to follow individual threads, trying many paths until we come to the one with which we resonate most strongly, the one we are meant for, and let other possibilities go.

Even though I always had the ability to hear dead people, I never imagined that being a medium would be my path. When I was younger I was certain I was going to be an actress; I loved performing and I was good at it. But as I got older I became more appreciative of the gift I'd been given; I found a lot of satisfaction in being able to help people who were grieving and found relief in the messages I could bring them. I still love goofing around to entertain my friends, but my aspirations to a career as an actress fell away eventually as I realized where I had a real contribution to make and saw how good that made me feel.

Karma

Probably the thing we think of first when we consider rebirth is the whole karma enchilada. Most people are familiar with this concept that our choices and actions will have future consequences. If our deeds are good, the fruits of our deeds will be positive; if our deeds are bad or harmful, we'll reap negativity. I like to think of it like a bank account. Any time we do something, whether positive or negative, we affect the balance of our karmic bank account. When we do the right thing even without any kind of appreciation or thanks or expectation of payment, we make a deposit, and our negative actions have an adverse effect on our balance, depleting our karmic account. Every moment of every day you are making either deposits or withdrawals. The idea is to keep making deposits—and never be overdrawn.

Karma is in play at every level of our lives, from the big agreements we make before coming here to the small choices we make every day. When you accumulate good karma there's no telling the ways in which you'll be rewarded.

I recently heard a story from a friend that was a great example of what we sometimes call "instant karma" (an immediate result or payback from something we've done). My friend was out with her cousin, having a couple drinks and visiting at a bar. Eventually they decided to call it a night and she asked for the check while they finished their wine. When she got it she didn't think it looked right— she'd thought it was going to be more than what the total said. She looked more closely and saw that the bartender had inadvertently left off their second glasses of wine. When she called the mistake to his attention the bartender thanked her and corrected the bill, which she then paid. Without looking she stuffed her wallet back in her bag, but she must have missed because a few minutes later as she and her cousin were just setting down their glasses to leave, a man tapped her on the shoulder and said, "Is this your wallet?" She said, "Concetta, talk about instant karma! That guy could easily have walked out with my wallet and I'd never have known where it went. Having the universe return it to me like that made me so happy that I'd done the right thing with the bartender."

Karma and Kids

I'm frequently asked about whether children have the same rules of karma as adults. I'll say more about that in the next chapter but will just touch on it here. In the Jewish religion it's not until a boy reaches the age of thirteen (twelve for girls) that they are "bound by the commandments," that is, they are ultimately responsible for their behavior and actions. I suppose it's like getting a free pass on some behaviors or mistakes up to that point, the kind of things kids do thoughtlessly. Which makes sense to me. According to brain scientists, this idea of ultimate responsibility should maybe come even later. The part of the human brain that has to do with making judgment calls, they say, isn't even fully developed until our early twenties. This is a biological fact of this physical plane and even before this discovery it was sufficiently clear that kids do dumb things, or even sometimes terrible things, as our legal system takes into account this immaturity when it distinguishes between adults and kids in the punishment meted out for certain crimes. I believe that even in the spiritual realm there is recognition and a distinction made between things kids do and things adults do. But nevertheless kids' actions do have karmic implications, spiritual implications, for this life and sometimes for others to come. There will have to be some sort of balancing or atonement for any negative actions. I'm certain that nearly every one of us has done something we're not proud of when we were only a child that we've reflected on many times throughout our lives. It may be that this memory in itself is something that keeps us from making other mistakes going forward. It's how we learn.

No Judgment, No Blame

Oftentimes, when we see someone in what could only be called heartbreaking circumstances we assume that person must have done something to deserve whatever their challenge may be. This is a common misconception about karma. We can never know another's true path and purpose. We can never make these assumptions and judgments based on outward appearances. An individual's Soul Contract is between that soul and God. Not every tough circumstance is the result of negative karma. Someone who appears unlucky may have willingly taken on a heavy burden in this lifetime for some higher purpose.

A soul may also be on some accelerated path. On occasion a soul may choose to challenge itself for the growth it will produce. Why would someone accept a physical limitation, an illness or injury, a terrible loss, a broken or dysfunctional family? A soul who wants to try a greater level of difficulty is like an Olympic diver challenging herself to a harder dive to get a higher score—a dive worth ten points instead of that easier one that's worth six.

Nor can you look at a situation and blame God—why would God let that person suffer? How could He allow this group to be persecuted and hurt? These individuals may be learning lessons, becoming polished or purified in some way. All—on a spiritual level—are willingly serving as examples, maybe to facilitate a lesson or advancement for others. The thing we *can* do when we see someone struggling with their burden is show compassion and try to help them with it. That furthers everyone and puts a nice deposit in your karmic bank.

Last of all, you can't judge or blame even yourself. Even as a psychic, there are things the Other Side keeps me from knowing about my own life. I'm here, just like you, having a human journey. Some of our life lessons will seem obvious to us. Some we may never be aware of until we cross back to the Other Side. Even if we are able to recall bits and pieces of our past lives we can't know it all; we can't know, for example, that we were some awful person who did so much harm and that's why we now have such a complicated and difficult life circumstance—as do millions and millions of people in the world at any given time. Ordinary souls take on extraordinary challenges in order to evolve spiritually and when we go back all the reasons are crystal clear. But not while we're here. We're not to judge; only God can judge.

Assistance from Our Guardian Angels

I want people to know that our deceased loved ones are our spirit guides, our personal angels. God wouldn't send us here to get a job done without giving us "staff." It may be a strange way to put it but our angels are like our personal "employees"; they are employees of our soul. Before we came here, the decision about who would be the perfect guardian angels to protect us was made with God, and He granted them permission to help. They might be individuals you knew well before they crossed, or they could even be people you've never met before in this lifetime but who have been near to you spiritually during other lifetimes. We go through this life here on earth with many defeats and many victories, and all the while our spirit guides walk with us. You wouldn't try to run a business without help. So don't try to run your business with God, that is, your life here, without the help of the guardian angels who were "hired" by God especially for you, to get you through this. Remember to pray for them, ask for their help, ask for God's help.

What can they do for us? They can help a "late bloomer" find her path by putting the right opportunities or people in her way. They can protect us from many kinds of danger. If you learn to listen for them when you are in a relaxed state they can spark a great idea that might help you with a project or an important discovery. Our angels might put us in the way of an opportunity to balance out some negative karma or even make a positive deposit in our karmic bank.

Success in earthly terms requires luck, connections, money, branding, credentials, and a big fat "maybe" (there's not even a guarantee). But success heaven-style only requires a willing heart that says, "I want to serve God." Through that opening, God will place around you the things you need, the people you need to get your spiritual work done. Heaven will provide for you what you need to succeed. When you show up with a willing heart, God will put everything in motion for you. You'll be in the right place at the right time, with the right opportunity and the right team.

Past-Life Residue

Once in a while we will have what we think of as a past-life memory, where we recall a past-life experience from the old body we once were in. I have a big front window that I see when I walk up and down the stairs in my house. That front window is wonderful during the day because I can see very clearly what's going by outside. But I live in the country, so at night, I don't see anything but pitch-black. And then, in the back of my mind, as I walk up or down those stairs, there's something that creeps me out about not knowing what's there in the dark. I've given this a lot of thought because I've wondered what it is that I'm worried about, what is it that I'm thinking, what puts me on edge. Suddenly I realized it's a past-life memory. I might have been a soldier and was shot in the back by someone I didn't see coming behind me. There are so many scenarios that could be possible. But the fact is there is something attached to my memory; something happened to me at another time, in another life, and now I have that ongoing feeling at night, that sense of something behind me that I'm uncomfortable about.

We all have these things that make us uncomfortable—seemingly irrational fears or phobias, or, conversely, things that somewhat inexplicably make us feel good. There are also good emotions and sensations attached to our buried past-life memories that may be stirred up by a present-day experience we have. Maybe a particular flower or scent reminds us of a place we used to call home in another life.

When we come back here, it's like we reach into the locker

where we hung up our fireman's coat on the Other Side and we bring that back with us. Sometimes we'll find ourselves doing similar things over several lifetimes, which makes the likelihood of having some memory of it or residual emotional tie with it stronger. Someone might say that they've had the natural ability to entertain all their life. If you get to the bottom of it they might tell you that ever since they were a kid they visualized themselves onstage or saw themselves singing or playing the piano. Or they'll feel a strong connection to a particular uniform—be it that fireman's coat or a suit of armor they wore last time they were here. But certainly every one of us has these things that are going on all the time. It may just be that not everyone will talk about it or admit it or look into what the possibilities are. And let's face it, the possibilities are endless.

Challenging for All

There is no one here who has an easy time all the time. There are those who have karmically earned a share of good fortune, if you will, and there are others here experiencing good fortune simply because it is their turn to experience this—what they make of it will either add to or subtract from their karmic account.

When I made my own Soul Contract, agreeing to come here and do the work I'm doing, obviously I had no idea what it would entail. Even after I was here and my ability had manifested, I still did not feel obliged to actually do the work. I asked for the ability to be quiet, to leave me alone. Later, as I got older, I wanted it to come back—but that was really because I thought it could help me personally in material ways, to get a better job or maybe find a great boyfriend. It wasn't until much later, and with some serious prodding by my deceased brother Harold from the Other

Side, that I was willing to do whatever was required of me in order to perform this service. Simply being able to hear souls speaking does not give me some special power to avert suffering. I'm often shown or told terrible things and there is nothing at all that I personally can do about them. What I can do is give people evidence that their loved ones are still with them, that life goes on in spirit after our physical death, that in essence and in fact, we are never alone.

Sometimes people hear what I'm saying and their reaction is, "Well, that's easy for you to say. Look at you—you've got it all going on." Yeah, it is easy for me to talk about this stuff even if it's not so easy for me to walk the talk. I have to make the same effort as any other human being. And the only reason it's easy for me to talk about it is that I've been in school for the past fifty-six years! This is what I have come to believe after years of listening to the souls. I live my life now with the comfort of knowing that I am at the very least on the right path. Time will tell.

It's important, even though what we set out to do here will be accomplished on the physical plane, earth, that we understand it in spiritual terms. What we do here in our physical body is really for the betterment of our soul, and given the fact that we are all connected with one ultimate universal purpose, for the betterment of all souls, if for any reason we do not accomplish what we have agreed to, there are no repercussions or punishments on the Other Side. God is not like Donald Trump sitting up on some cloud saying, "You're fired!" The individual soul itself may experience a brief sense of regret, or, with the realization that they not only did not fulfill their agreement but also actually harmed someone or something, the soul may need a period of healing on the Other Side before it is ready to try again. But there is no clock running on the soul's journey, no limit to the number of times they can try again. God will set up different circumstances for us over and over again until we get it. That soul will have as many subsequent lifetimes here as are necessary for it to eventually perfect its understanding that we are all one with God, filled with His love and made to be cocreators with Him forever.

Our coming to this plane in order to get closer to God is like Dorothy going to Oz to learn lessons of the heart in order to return to her family who loves her in Kansas. Without leaving home our perspective is limited. Not until we have left home many times can we truly know home, know the perfection of God. We have to leave and return, leave and return, each time widening our perspective, seeing things from a different angle. We need experience of every religion, culture, ethnic background; we have to come full circle and see God from all sides.

The inventor and statesman Benjamin Franklin was a lifelong believer in reincarnation. When he was just in his early twenties he wrote for himself an amusing, if lengthy, epitaph in which he compares himself to a book that will be stripped of its bindings and become "food for worms" (bookworms maybe), but which will eventually be "revised and corrected by the author" and come out as a "more elegant edition." As an old man, his belief still held. He wrote, "When I see nothing annihilated and not a drop of water wasted, I cannot suspect the annihilation of souls, or believe that [God] will suffer the daily waste of millions of minds ready made that now exist, and put Himself to the continual trouble of making new ones. Thus, finding myself to exist in the world, I believe I shall, in some shape or other, always exist . . ." I would love to have known Ben Franklin, and given our many, many lives here, the reality is that I may have!

Reminders and Practices

Meditation and prayer are the two spiritual power tools that anyone can use to help them with their earth journey and to fulfill their Soul Contract.

- Meditate to find your path and purpose. Sit quietly, empty your mind, and see what hints you are given.

- Pray for self-knowledge, to know you are on the right path and to know you are doing the right thing in any challenging circumstance.

- Pray for assistance from your spirit guides any time you need them!

Mission Entities and Mystical Travelers

There is a crack in everything, that's how the light gets in.
—Leonard Cohen

Not everyone who returns to earth comes with a specific mission from God, but those who do are very logically called "Mission Entities." All souls who are Mission Entities could be called, in earth terms, "spiritual seekers." This leaning will have been embedded in them since birth. A Mission Entity's parents may recognize their child as being interested in spiritual matters from an early age, or this leaning may be dormant at first and then some event in their life will cause it to awaken in them, but all Mission Entities do have this nature. Their role here varies, but all, in some way, are here to facilitate a correction, to help bring about a necessary change that reaches beyond their immediate circle of family and friends. Often their mission will require a great sacrifice; sometimes it may even require that their death be an example or be some kind of catalyst so others can see things in a different way. A Mission

Entity is not concerned with self-improvement or with enriching themselves in human terms. Since the physical plane in general resists change, they will naturally face challenges, and their lives may be comprised of great highs and lows.

In spiritual terms, we would regard these souls as "perfected," as having earned the right to never come back here again, but instead they have selflessly agreed to return to this very difficult place simply to uplift other souls and help accelerate their spiritual journey. Rarely do these souls come here in the guise of a saint. They may be young or old when they die and return to the Other Side, they may rise to fame here or be known only to a few, but their actions here will cause ripples outward. Their work here is necessary to our human evolution as well as our spiritual growth.

The Death of a Child

Sometimes our loved ones cross at a time that seems to us way too early. Maybe they are young adults or even just young children. The ones left behind are hit hardest; the loss is so difficult to understand and come to terms with. Occasionally, even when it's an older person who crosses, we have the feeling that it was not yet their time because they were so good, doing so much good for others. It's especially hard when a child is lost. The truth is, no death is "untimely." Even suicide is not untimely because at some level that individual has made a choice. What we think of as untimely for the person who crosses really is untimely for those of us who are still here. That soul leaves either because their work here is completed or it is their perception that their work would be impossible for them to complete even if they were to stay. The sooner they go home, the sooner they can get a fresh start. They are ready to go home. The Other Side is the place of perfection and renewal, of God, love, and forgiveness. We are the ones who are not ready.

Nevertheless, a child's death is always tragic in human terms. I was giving a reading for a woman who told me her grandson, Nick, had died. I was able to bring Nick to her and then had to ask, "Why do I see two Nicks?" and she confirmed that his father's name was also Nick and he was deceased, too. The grandmother had been wrestling with why God would take such a young boy; how could God do this?

Opening the Heart

We need to understand that free will is always in force. A Mission Entity is a soul who chooses to come here with a full plate. As I said, they are very advanced and know that if they take on what in earth terms is a heavy burden they will push forward the evolution of many souls because the Soul Link Group among which they have lived many lifetimes is not just family but also friends, work associates, neighbors, the community, any number of connections by contact. Out of love and sacrifice they come and take on a life that may involve some debilitating illness or condition, some kind of injustice, or sometimes an "early" death. Usually they are talented, have more than what the average person has, and then they are taken. A five-year-old child can make such a difference in so many lives that it's like they've actually lived fifty years. What makes a child a Mission Entity is the power of their influence upon many people, known and unknown, during their short life and even after they have gone back to God. When a child dies they are a teacher in that family, karmically placed in the lives of all the family's relatives and friends. Their function is to give the family (and others) the opportunity to advance more rapidly in their spiritual development. When a child dies, hearts are broken, but in a sense they are also *broken open*, which allows greater receptivity, or as Leonard Cohen said, it allows the Light to come in. A pathway is created, an opening in the heart chakra. What I have seen in my own work is that in most such cases those closest to the child will be actively searching for answers to what seems to them an unjust death; they become seekers even if they were not seekers before. Even though it's painful, grief can create such an opening in the heart that it allows for truly revolutionary evolution and growth, albeit in a way that a person probably would never have signed up for. So these children, these Mission Entities, are karmic teachers, here to teach us lessons in many ways, to help us "get" our lessons. They may change many people (a Soul Link group may be made up of two or three hundred souls or more), or just one or a few who need it most. They come on a mission from God, with God's help. An agreement is made on the Other Side and a plan is made to bring about a situation that will hopefully effect a desired change in soul and spirit. Some people go through life never realizing the simple things about themselves that could help them lead a better, more loving, more fulfilled life. They may have come back numerous times without grasping very basic lessons. A Mission Entity might come to help them learn to do it a different way this time, enable them to graduate to the next lesson—and, via the domino effect, could also touch many others.

> *My name is Caitlyn, I am 20 years old, living in Chicago. I have never been a skeptic, as my grandmother has always been really into readings and things of that nature. In the last year I have lost two very close friends to very unexplainable deaths. I just refused to accept straight death as an answer. I knew there had to be more.*

I wasn't looking when I stumbled upon your books either! Every-
thing happens for a reason. You have helped me answer so many
questions. I now have hope and a greater outlook on life here on
earth. Thank you so very much for doing what you do! You're a
beautiful person with a wonderful soul. ♥

Whether a soul crosses back to the Other Side as a child (and here I mean a "child" in earth terms, because in spiritual terms the person we perceive as a child will be a very old, very evolved soul) or as an older person, in the eternal scheme of things, we are only here a short time. Mother Teresa was not a young woman in earth terms when she returned to God, and yet she was surely aware of how short her time was here and had to be satisfied knowing that her job was to begin the work that would continue after she left. The way we think about time here is very artificial; we've created schedules—minutes, hours, days, weeks, years—to keep our business here running smoothly, create community-building rituals like holidays, mark world events and personal ones like birthdays and anniversaries. But what matters in spiritual terms is not the length of time we are on this side of the veil, but the impact of our lives here—the growth we experience, the lessons we share with others, the love we give. Some of us will make an impact on the lives of hundreds, others thousands or millions. How long we are here to accomplish that is irrelevant.

My name is Olivia Ramos, I'm 28 years old and I'm from Aca-
pulco, Gro. Mexico. Three years ago my nephew Bryan died. He
was seven years old and he was a beautiful baby. He'd been born
with hydro encephala and espina bifida and he didn't walk. He
was so special. My family always thought that Bryan was an

angel that God permitted to live with us for a few years. I miss him a lot, and my heart hurts. Many times I begged God to let him live longer. I just want to hold and kiss him and tell him how much I miss him. Sometimes I dream about him, but when I remember he's dead I wake up.

I remember the day before Bryan's death in the hospital in Mexico City he told my sister and me that he would never forget us. He took our hands and promised us we'd always be a family and he told us he'd always be with us. We cried, knowing that Bryan was saying good-bye to us.

When I read your book I feel comforted because I know that my Bryan is with God and now he can walk and he can run— that makes me very happy! Concetta, really you are blessed by God. I would really be happy if you come to Mexico so I can meet you and ask for my precious nephew Bryan Arcos Ramos!

A Mission Entity is a pure soul and can be very vulnerable. There are many misinterpretations about Mission Entities. They're not necessarily involved in some classically spiritual endeavor. They can be in any walk of life, wearing any face. There are many in the music world. For example, Jimi Hendrix was one, as were Hank Williams, Janis Joplin, and Kurt Cobain. So are the Beatles—all of the Beatles; each one of them contributed to this side in different ways. They helped to change the world, our attitudes toward our differences, as well as the ways we think about love and peace and hope. Each one of them has had a special influence on us. Jim Morrison, who even said, "No one here gets out alive," was a great teacher about death. Even Michael Jackson and other gifted individuals like him change the way we think because their music changes the way we feel and express ourselves. There is an infinite number of things that can do this—things we choose to study, things we read, things we're exposed to. But music goes directly to our core and touches the soul faster than reading any book.

Mystical Travelers

There are many Mission Entities. There are fewer Mystical Travelers. These are even more evolved beings who are completely unconditional. I sometimes think of them as God's astronauts—they know that this visit to "Camp Earth" is so brief, and eternity and goodness and paradise and who you are as an individual are so expansive, beyond what humans can comprehend, and they will sacrifice entering into a body for a brief time to take on what seems to be an immeasurable amount of pain, because they will then influence the masses beyond any individual Soul Link Group.

A Mission Entity can be understood best as a single highly evolved soul, but explaining the Mystical Traveler is a little trickier. The Mystical Traveler is actually a very highly evolved consciousness, acting through another soul (a container) here on earth. In a sense, this consciousness is a "teacher in residence" within that soul, and the soul container is always someone who is willing to learn more, someone who is seeking and wants to be of greater help to others. The Mystical Traveler is pure spirit, pure light even, immune to the law of karma. The human individual through which this spirit works will usually take on some challenge—often something physical as a reminder to stay in the body. You can think of the perfection of this soul as a hot air balloon that would drift away without some ballast—a chronic illness, a physical imperfection maybe—to anchor it here. They come here to help people change their attitudes, often, but not always, specifically about love, the spiritual plane, or death and dying. I realize this idea of another consciousness inhabiting a soul can sound like "demonic possession." It is the farthest thing from this. The soul host is always willing and has agreed to this in advance. It is actually "angelic cooperation."

Mystical Travelers are totally selfless beings. We can name famous ones like Gandhi, Mother Teresa, Matthew Stepanek—when he died of a form of muscular dystrophy at only fourteen years of age he had already published six books of poetry and was an ambassador both for his disease and for world peace! At twelve, he had already met and discussed world peace with Jimmy Carter. That is not a common twelve-year-old. Ryan White is another example. His death from AIDS raised world awareness of this terrible disease.

A very different example is someone like Princess Diana, who seemed to be very powerful. She appeared beyond reach, untouchable, totally insulated within the royal family. People didn't know her reality. But once people learned of her bulimia, her loneliness, her marital problems, she became very ordinary. Very vulnerable. That is a Mystical Traveler; she will endure in our memory because she touched millions and millions of people with her story, as well as helped others with her humanitarian work trying to rid the world of land mines that have killed and maimed so many. A Down syndrome child whose name you may not even know but whose innate blessed nature is clear to anyone who sees him or her also is most often a Mystical Traveler. The Mystical Traveler comes to this plane knowing they will suffer beyond what the average or even above average individual can handle. The work done here may be grand (in appearance) or humble (in appearance) but the most humble will have grand effects, and the most grand will also touch the humble masses. Because they are never out of reach of the Other Side, it is almost like the entire time they are here they are channeling the energy from there. They may not know it in their conscious mind, but at the level of Soul Consciousness they certainly are aware.

There can be some confusion as to differences between Mission Entities and Mystical Travelers since there is overlap in the way these types of souls appear to others. Not all are famous. They might be an ordinary person who through their actions or their suffering reaches many millions of people, around the world. And there also is, I believe, some blending of the two in some individuals. I believe my brother Harold, for instance, was both. Along with others, he agreed to come here as a gay man in the 1960s, an incredibly difficult challenge because of the deep prejudice against homosexuals at this time when these folks were finally trying to get out of their dark, soul-imprisoning closets. Those difficulties were compounded by the epidemic of AIDS that began in the 1980s and so decimated this community, a disease that Harold contracted. The disease itself is devastating, and the prejudice and condemnation that these people suffered along with living with the symptoms of the disease were horrific. But he endured it all, never losing his beautiful spirit—no one who came in contact with him could possibly think he was a bad person. Through the example of his very existence it was obvious to anyone that a homosexual could be a good person, and a person with AIDS could be a good person. (Harold also cared for, loved, and raised two boys, half-white and half-black, whose father was in prison for murder. And I have heard innumerable stories from other people of the kindnesses Harold showed them, how they were changed by him.)

Ryan White, another Mystical Traveler, was a hemophiliac

who contracted HIV-AIDS via a transfusion. Ryan was not gay, but the gay community was vital in providing his family with the best information for treatment. His mother stated, "I hear mothers today say they're not going to work with no gay community. . . . When it comes to your son's life you better start changing your heart and your attitude around." This was his burden, this was his gift—he suffered to change others, to help them evolve.

My brother was beaten and kicked and left for dead in a snow-bank simply for being who he was. Thirty years later, Matthew Shepard was tortured and killed for being gay. In another thirty years, what will it mean to agree to come here as a homosexual? I hope these souls have not sacrificed for nothing. I hope their work means the hardest times are done and "gay" really will mean "gay"! And not just gay but also free.

The Mystical Traveler influences us in an infinite number of ways. Jimi Hendrix influenced the world with his music, his skin color, his struggle with addiction. My brother Harold loved Jimi and always had his music playing on his stereo, so I can't help thinking of Harold any time I hear Jimi's music. Jimi was here for a short time but he smashed so many boundaries. He touched millions in his time and he continues to affect new people who were not even on this side when he was as they hear his music and come to know his story, which had tragedy but also true gran-deur and nobility and absolute joy. He and his music embodied and transmitted messages of love, peace, harmony, and freedom. Even the clothes he wore symbolized something as boundless as our true spirits. Though many millions have been touched by him and his music over the last fifty years—and will be forever, going forward—each of us will have only a piece of his purpose. Only God and Jimi will ever know the entire agreement between them.

More Are Entering

At the present time we are hosting many more Mission Entities and Mystical Travelers than have been the norm in the past. They are not "messiahs," per se, and would certainly shun that term if it were applied to them, but they do have a messianic mission. They don't care about the "self" or getting personal recognition. On the other side of the veil, they do get full appreciation and credit for their mission. They could be someone in a research lab who has a very powerful scientific ability applied to stem cell research, understanding the connection of biology and technology, working for a breakthrough. Each has been sent here by God and comes with passion.

A man came to see me and told me he had an eight-year-old son by a second marriage (and had two children by his first marriage). He told me, "Concetta, I never believed in an afterlife or that we could talk with the dead—any of these things that I now know are true." He said, "I read your book because I wanted more information. But it wasn't your book that brought me to the realization. It was my own son." He went on to tell me that from the time his son could talk, he realized there was something very different about him; there was something he was trying to tell him and his wife. His wife was actually frightened by what was clearly different about their child. The boy seemed to know how frightened his mother was and so tended to confide most in his father. From the time he could talk he talked about the "other place." He'd say things like, "Dad, Mommy doesn't understand, but the other place is so much easier; this place is so hard." In reality the mother was terribly afraid because she believed this connection he had meant that he was going to die.

Sometimes father and son would go to the cemetery to visit

the grave of the father's parents, who had died long before the boy was born. This child recalled knowing both the man's parents and recalled all sorts of details that of course he had no earthly way of knowing, and he would refer to them by their first names. When the man asked his son, "How do you know this?" the child replied, "Because I knew them, from the other place." One time they visited the cemetery around Christmastime and lots of graves had been adorned with wreaths and flowers and other sorts of decorations of the season. The boy was upset because his grandparents didn't have anything on their grave and they had not thought to bring anything with them to leave. So the little boy took off his mittens and insisted on leaving them on his grandparents' grave. He put them there and said, "Daddy, I want Clare [his grandmother] to have this." They left the cemetery, leaving the mittens there on the grave. About a month later they returned, and the mittens were gone. Over to the side of the cemetery was a huge pile of debris—grave blankets, wreaths, old flowers, crosses, etc., all kinds of stuff that had been cleaned up. When they were still at a distance, the boy noticed the mittens were gone from his grandparents' grave and became frantic. He headed for the pile, ostensibly to look for them, but his father stopped him, saying, "Son, please don't be upset. You're never going to find them in all that." The boy said, "They shouldn't have taken them. They belonged to Clare." The man managed to calm his son down and they continued toward the grave. Suddenly, the boy took off running. The man chased after his son, saying, "What's the matter? Where are you going?" The boy stopped in front of a big old tree whose branches split in the middle. The boy reached up into the split and pulled out the mittens. The man looked at his son in total disbelief and asked, "How on earth did you know that the mittens were there?" His son said, "Clare told me." They returned to the grave and replaced the mittens. When they were leaving, the groundskeeper came up to the man and his son and said, "Oh, I'm so glad I found you. I noticed that your son left his mittens on your parents' grave. I didn't want to throw them away so I found a place to hide them where I knew they'd be safe. I want to tell you where they are."

The man responded, "It's not necessary. My son already found them."

"He found them?" the groundskeeper asked. "How is that possible? I put them up in a tree, deep between the branches."

The man said, "I don't know. My son seems to know a lot of things I can't explain."

On another visit to the cemetery the boy told his father, "Clare wishes that Dale were here with them." "Concetta," he said, "that's when I completely lost it. My son would have no way of knowing that my mother had a child who only lived a few months, before I was born. His name was Dale. He was a crib-death baby, and he isn't buried at the same cemetery as my mother and father. I lost it at that point because I realized that my son was onto something that none of us could understand or explain. I have been searching for answers and searching for information so that I can communicate with my son in a more informed way. My wife is a little frightened, but she's getting on board."

I don't know what may be in store in this child's future. I don't know what his work will turn out to be or what it will require of him. But children like this, Mission Entities or sometimes Mystical Travelers, are showing up in more and more places around the world. The veil between here and the Other Side is getting thinner and thinner and the glory of God surrounds us. We need to pay attention, wherever we are—at work, socializing, walking around at a shopping mall. These kids are being born into families like this man's. He had no belief or understanding or education on this subject, but because of his true love and compassion he is willing to listen to his son, instead of blowing him off, and really try to understand and get answers.

The Pain of Spiritual Growth

Because a particular mission may be accomplished in a relatively brief time here, a soul returning home when its work is done can mean the death of a young person. What does this mean for those of us who directly experience such a loss, regardless of the reasons of that special individual for taking on such a mission? Even if we understand intellectually that it is their choice to render this type of spiritual service and it is intended to enable us (and others) to evolve spiritually, it is still tremendously painful to lose someone dear to us.

In the aftermath of any such event—a young person's crossing—it's of paramount importance how the mother acts. She has a choice. When other children and a husband/father are involved, they won't survive if the mother makes the wrong choice. If she takes to her bed, depressed, unable to get up or show interest in life or her remaining children, the family will be destroyed. I say it's up to the mother only because most often it is the mother who has the skill set for holding these relationships together; men are notoriously bad about expressing their feelings and it would be more typical for a man to hold in everything he's feeling and close out other family members unless the mother can set an example for all. If the mother makes the right choice, the family can move forward and heal—and not just the family, but also the friends the deceased has left behind. She can really set that example that will show others how to respond positively and not allow this terrible loss to ruin their lives. If she is brave, others will be affected by her bravery. She will inspire and encourage them.

The concern is that the mother may feel that she is not honoring the child who has crossed if she appears to be "okay" and attempts to move forward in a positive way. I do understand how she might struggle with feelings of guilt. But the Other Side has told us, over and over again, that guilt is such a worthless emotion, a trap even. She has to ignore any of those kinds of feelings in order to do what is right for her family. If the mother chooses to live in pain, grief, guilt, anger—all those terrible emotions—not only does she not contribute to healing the family, but she also risks cutting off family and friends from herself. There is nothing anyone here can do about such a loss; they can't return the child to life. So, in frustration, they may simply begin to avoid the mother, which in itself creates a domino effect, making her pain more real, more justifiable. It's terribly difficult—I do not in any way minimize how hard it is to get past this type of loss. But if she can gather the necessary courage to lead in healing, there is—I promise you—much joy to still be had in her life.

I don't really mean to put all this exclusively on the mother. As I said, it usually falls to her to set the example because in most cases she is the emotional head of the family, and typically men have more difficulty in this area. But there are families with just a dad, and in that case, were something like this to happen, he'd be the one who'd have to step up. There's always one to whom everyone else looks for an example of how to behave. In some circumstances, it might be a school principal who has to try to provide a context for what has happened so that their students can feel secure and keep moving forward in a positive way. For that matter, it might be *you* who has this job; maybe you are the one who is best equipped.

In all my years as a medium, I've met with many parents who have lost children and it's going to go one way or the other, depending on the choice the parent makes. I saw this with my own parents when my brother died, how it affected my mother and father. When my brother Harold died, it was truly amazing to watch how my mother responded. She was used to disappointment, tragedy, and pain due to her early upbringing. She had already lived through hell and survived to tell the tale. I believe she made a decision early in life that she wanted to be happy and enjoy whatever she could possibly enjoy while she was here. Losing her son must have been the most difficult challenge and yet she kept her head high and gave love to all the mourners. She lived with his memory with a smile on her face, knowing that that's what he'd have wanted her to do. This amazed me all my life.

Healing comes in different forms and no two people will find it in the same way. But it is important to search, to seek relief. Some may gain understanding by talking with others in the same situation—a support group. Some may seek therapy, maybe looking for "permission" to recover and move forward. To some, their church, mosque, or temple is the greatest comfort. Everybody is changed forever, one way or another. I urge anyone who has been broken in this way to try to let the Light come in. You can choose to be present and loving to your family here who need you and love you, or you can focus on the loss, on the hole in your life, and wind up destroying yourself and everyone who has feelings for you. It's important that you make the right choice.

Even if we do not have a larger mission, we all have lessons we are here to learn. We die at the appropriate time. We die when our work is done. This is what you need to know when you lose a child: They had finished their job here. If we are still here it's because we have not yet achieved our purpose. Is this easy to accept? No. I know it isn't. But this is the understanding we must come to if we are to find peace. We need to continue our own work joyfully—not mechanically going through the motions here in a state of grief, withholding our love and our energy from others, or worse, polluting the energy of others. Sadness is to be expected but not held on to. Don't allow yourself to feel guilty about healing. It takes time, but laugh as often as you can, smile as often as you can. I promise you it will get easier. Remember you are never alone—the spirit of your loved one is with you always.

Reminders and Practices

- Open your eyes and open your heart—allow yourself to be inspired by those who are doing the heavy lifting here. If you know someone like this (you do!), thank them.

- If you have known and loved a Mission Entity who has returned home, consider whether it is right for you to help carry forward the work they've begun. Maybe this means rolling up your sleeves or maybe it means starting some sort of foundation that will support their cause.

- If you are a true seeker, open your mind and heart to Mystical Traveler consciousness. Give it permission to work through you.

People Who Need People

Always, Sir, set a high value on spontaneous kindness. He whose inclination prompts him to cultivate your friend-ship of his own accord will love you more than one whom you have been at pains to attach to you.

—Samuel Johnston

A family is a place where minds come in contact with one another. If these minds love one another, the home will be as beautiful as a flower garden. But if these minds get out of harmony with one another it is like a storm that plays havoc with the garden.

—Buddha

Human relationships can be the most nerve-wracking, annoying, hurtful, hilarious, comforting, and joy-producing things on this planet. Other people bring us our greatest challenges and our greatest rewards. I'll say it over and over: We are all one here, all connected and all a part of God. Yet when we are on this side our consciousness is attached to a physical body to provide the illusion of separateness. Other people are the cast of characters we work with as we face obstacles, learn lessons, balance our karma, and find understanding in this big play of life.

Soul Link Groups

Due to the veil of forgetting we are subject to here, we usually don't recall all the relationships we've shared in past lives. The forgetting is important. If we were able to remember our past lives in full detail there would be more of a compulsion, I believe, to dwell on them to the point where we weren't accomplishing what we need to accomplish in this life. We're not intended to compare. The consciousness we arrive here with is the sum distillation of all our other lives; it's the base of understanding that we operate from now. If we have worked on our lessons in previous lifetimes our understanding will be greater from the outset. We may not "get" everything, but we'll have a good start to work from.

Even though we don't remember, it remains a fact that anyone who is in our life today has been in our life before. We all return here in Soul Link Groups that can be quite large—there really is no limit to the number of souls in such a group. We've been together many times before, over many lifetimes, and will be together again. Our Soul Link Group is not just our family or extended family but also those we work with; those whom we encounter throughout our day; the folks we see at our temple, mosque, or church; the person who scans our groceries or hands us our dry-cleaning; that person next to us on the plane—all like circles rippling outward.

You can think of a Soul Link Group as a repertory theater

troupe—we all take turns playing different roles, with heroes and villains, crime and redemption, love, loss, and laughter in every production. We each may have a different dominant nature and get "typecast" in similar roles over several lifetimes, but we all, over time, get a chance to try different characters. In fact switching roles is absolutely necessary and the main reason we come back here over and over—to learn the joys and sorrows of our fellow beings, to gain compassion, to spiritually evolve through different perspectives, different experiences. Within each Soul Link Group there is an incalculable number of overlapping productions going on simultaneously. The individual who plays a minor role in the show you are starring in will be center stage in his or her own production at the same time, and you are a minor character in many such productions at once. It's important that we bear this in mind. You never know when someone playing an incidental character in your show may be upgraded to a lead—or you may be given a larger role in *their* show. As the saying goes, "There are no small parts, only small actors." And the directors and producers are all on the Other Side!

The way the human mind is built, with a somewhat limited range of focus at any given time, makes us more aware of our closer relationships, the "inner circle" of family and friends. But our relationships are not only one-to-one, but also Soul Link Group–to–Soul Link Group. As we develop spiritually we need to learn to expand our focus, sharing our energy and our love not only with an individual or with relatives and friends, but eventually with all those in the world. We are made of energy; there is energy between us and energy contained in our every interaction. Energy can heal or harm through a comforting act or an unkind word. Our family and friends, in a sense, are like a training ground where we rehearse our energetic exchanges at close range and see, "Oh, when I do this, they do that. When I say this, they feel like that. So if I want this effect, I need to be this way." Then we take the show on the road, so to speak.

Family

"You can pick your friends but you can't pick your family." According to everything I've been told by the Other Side, this old saying is not true! Since we are here to learn lessons and we learn by being challenged, very few have what they would call a perfect "Beaver Cleaver" 1950s television sitcom family. But, hard as it may be to accept, we do have the perfect family and circumstances for our spiritual purposes. They are perfect for what you are here to learn and what you are here to teach—they are the characters you need to play with and play against. And even if you've forgotten, you picked them out before coming here.

Families can be a tangled mass of karmic energies. If your Soul Link Group has already done a lot of spiritual work over many lifetimes, there may be more true harmony among the individuals, but an illusion of calm can also prevail when feelings are simply being suppressed, energy withheld—it looks like peace to the outside eye, but within the group there is tension and unease. Sometimes the main family unit is in such agreement over their dysfunction that any dissenter—one who calls out the dysfunction—is regarded as the black sheep! Ironically, that individual may be the main teacher in that family, even if they are the youngest child.

Like everything else on this side of the veil, families are stressed by physical, earth-plane realities. It takes a lot of intention and positive energy to hold such a unit together over time. Any closeness felt within a family is due to the contribution of energy by its various members. This closeness can be positive or negative depending upon the words and actions through which the energy is conveyed. So just because a family is close it's not necessarily conducive to spiritual harmony, and an excess of negative energy in close confines can cause explosions.

Ideally, the family unit will be a repository of loving energy, shared among all members, providing the stability for each to do their work in the world and providing a place of refuge and healing when needed. But if family members don't invest their energy in the family unit, the bonds will be weak and the family can disconnect. It may be that energy is being expended elsewhere—this happens naturally as a child grows up and leaves the family nest. But if a parent is constantly away from home, whether working or more focused on other relationships, it weakens the family unit. I don't in any way mean to suggest that a parent working to feed their family is actually weakening the family. But if absences are long then more effort needs to be made to keep lines of connection and communication in good repair.

Mother and Child

All family members have karma between them, but a mother's karmic connection to her child is usually especially strong and with each child the connection will be unique. The karmic connection between a mother and a child could be a million different things. They may have been in a previous relationship with a lot of problems and turmoil, so they are here this time to work out the pain and grief of the previous failure—this could be an opportunity for the soul who is "playing the mother" this time around to nurture a soul they previously mistreated. Or it could have been a loving relationship filled with peace and harmony and this time they've come to learn something new or to help others with something they've already learned. These relationships are often not straightforward and can take some unraveling even when we sincerely want to understand what makes them tick. Due to the media as well as stories we've heard since childhood we have an idea of the "traditional" relationship between parent and child, but we need to bear in mind that each of us is just a soul—we're not always a specific kind of soul. There's no such thing as a mother soul, a father soul, etc. so a soul who is your parent in this lifetime may never have acted this role before and might not be that great in this part. How often have you seen a child in a family step up and look after things that a parent can't seem to handle?

I feel certain that I was with my mother before this life and that we had a hard time previously. From childhood and for many years I was confused by her personality and ways. It took nearly a lifetime for me to understand what was at the root of the issues we had between us when I was younger. What I came to understand was that to some degree my mother was trying to live her missed childhood (from this time around) through mine. Being raised in an orphanage where she was mistreated and deprived of basic love, decent clothes, and decent food, and was made to perform tasks such as cleaning a hallway as if there were to be surgery performed in it—with a nun coming behind her with a white glove, no less—it's unsurprising that she had no idea how to be a mother. She didn't know how to make a meal or take care of a home or celebrate holidays like a family would. She enjoyed my growing up and wanted to join in, more like a friend than a parent. I wanted a mother, not a friend, and I resented her for this, even though I loved her deeply. My mother is someone who would give anything to anybody who asked because things had no value to her. And she would laugh with or befriend anyone. All she wanted was to be loved. I just didn't understand. I still don't have every answer to my questions about our relationship but this much at least is clear to me and I do recognize the power the relationship had.

Dear Concetta,

I just can't thank you enough for the wonderful peace you gave me on June 7, 2010. My husband is also at peace. I let him hear the tape from the reading when I got home. It set him free. You were so right, he had a horrible childhood. I have been taking the brunt of it for 43 years of marriage.

I noticed all the pictures you have in your waiting area. I'm not famous but I'm sending you my picture in great love and a feeling of thanks for allowing me to be less angry at my husband and make his final days happy.

New Arrivals

Any Soul Link Group will be partially split between those on this side and those on the Other Side at any given time. Those on the Other Side are there to help us in any way they can with the challenges we face here until it is their turn to come back. When it's time, with God's guidance and assistance, that soul will choose their parents and birth circumstances and join us over here. The circumstances they choose may be unconventional, but we have to trust that they know what they are doing.

A client I'd done a reading for a few years ago was visiting with me again. She said, "Concetta, can I tell you about the last reading you did for me? It really changed my life." Since I'm pretty much in an altered state when I'm talking with the souls, when I hear these stories from clients, either in person or in a letter they send me, about something I've told them that has turned out to be true or has helped them in some way, it's really news to me. In this case she told me that she'd come to see me several years earlier and I told her that her daughter was going to be having a baby. She had sighed and said that this was highly unlikely unless her daughter adopted. Her daughter, she said, had been married for fifteen years and was then forty-five years old, so the family had pretty much stopped thinking that there would be children from the marriage. I'd told her, "Well, adoption is a beautiful thing, but I believe this baby is going to be born to your daughter and it's going to be a boy." Needless to say, she was skeptical. But when she went home she called her daughter and told her about the reading. She said, "Concetta says you're going to have a baby boy."

"Really," said her daughter, not even seeming curious, and just left it at that.

A couple weeks later it was my client's wedding anniversary and her daughter handed her an anniversary card. When she opened it up and read the inscription it said, "Your grandson will be here in seven months." She had been pregnant and knew it when her mother had called her but hadn't wanted to give away the surprise quite yet!

As I told this woman, adoption, too, is a beautiful thing, and make no mistake, in the case of adoption, the child who is brought into a new family was always a part of that Soul Link Group. As are the child's biological parents—even if they live far away or in another country. (Someone's having a different nationality than yours does not mean they are not in the same Soul Link Group as you.) In earthly terms a new relationship is created when a child is adopted into a new family, but all were together before and will be together again.

It used to be that laws in many states prevented adopted kids from discovering who their biological parents were. Children are given up or left parentless for any number of reasons and of course this was intended to protect the privacy of the individuals who had given up the child. But the result was often lifelong questioning and grief on the part of the child, or on both sides. In spiritual terms this was like a forced disconnection from some part of the Soul Link Group (even though the adoptive parents were also Soul Link Group members). These laws are changing now, albeit too slowly in my opinion, allowing for reconnection and healing. My assistant Elena's husband, Troy, is adopted. His brother is his parents' biological son. Troy has now found his biological mother, and they are now one big happy family. Every one of these players has known each other over past lives and now they are reunited in this one.

Friends

If you have good friends you can survive any family.

Families often present us with the greatest karmic challenges we'll face in any given life. The souls who make up our family may be more or less spiritually evolved. We may have parents who are well meaning but self-absorbed or emotionally absent, leaving us feeling abandoned, and our task may be to overcome this and not re-create a similar dynamic in a new relationship that is undemanding but unfulfilling. Friction might be set up among siblings who have to vie for parental attention. We may find ourselves in a family situation that is outright abusive. Along the way, our greatest ally is a good friend, most often steered our way by the Other Side.

I met my best friend, Mushy, when we were just in grade school. In spite of other little girls telling each of us that the other didn't like her, the Other Side was telling me something quite different. One day when I was riding my bike I passed Mushy as she waited outside a bar for her father to come out. I waved but pedaled on by—until I heard a voice say, "Go back. She waved." I did, and that was the start of a lifelong friendship.

Over close to fifty years, Mushy and I have been together through thick and thin. I was lucky to have a loving family; my parents adored Mushy and my home became a haven for her when her own parents were being abusive. I was glad to be there for her in those days and through a couple of relationships that didn't work out. At the same time, Mushy taught me things I'd never learned from my mother—how to do my hair, how to pick out an outfit, even how to clean the house (no one cleans a house better than Mushy—she is German after all!). Most of all, she kept me from diving off the deep end when I was having such difficulty with my husband, John, and his family in the early years of my marriage.

Stay Open

As we get older we may think we know who all our friends are, but we need to stay open to the possibility that we have not yet met someone who will turn out to be incredibly important to us. Our lives can be changed on a dime by some powerful soul entering at any moment.

My old friend Debbie Malanga had a cousin who had attended some of my shows in the past. I had already validated certain things for her, but there had been nothing in particular that made me remember her, so the fact that Debbie kept saying to me, "You need to meet my cousin Ginger," wasn't making the impression that maybe it should have. It was just when things were beginning to take off with my public career and it seemed like there were a lot of people who wanted to meet me at that point, so I didn't have any idea whether meeting Debbie's cousin was something really important or whether she was just another person who had heard of me or maybe had come to a show and wanted to meet me "in person." So I was saying to Debbie, "Who is she? What does she want to meet me for?"

What I didn't know was that it was Ginger prompting Debbie. Ginger (a psychotherapist and spiritual teacher) kept having this very strong feeling about me, and Ginger is someone who has learned over the course of her life to pay attention to her feelings—especially the ones that don't go away. She had a sense that there was something big in front of me and she wanted to do my astrological chart. Ginger's about my age, maybe a couple years older, and she has studied astrology since she was fifteen years old, so let's just say, for many years this has been her passion. So finally it was arranged that I'd meet Ginger at her office.

At the time Ginger had her little Maltese, Nino Giuseppe; her parents had already crossed. Nino used to go to the office with Ginger every day. When clients would come, Nino would get up and greet them, then return to his crate and go back to sleep. Now, an hour before I was to arrive at Ginger's office, Nino got out of his crate and stood staring up toward the corner of the ceiling between Ginger's chair and the client's chair, barking and barking for a solid hour. Ginger was so concerned, she picked him up and checked him all over to see if there was anything wrong with him; she took him outside twice to see if he maybe needed to go out and was just showing it in some weird way. She gave him a treat. Nothing calmed him down. Nino's a really good dog so this was very strange behavior. Ginger had no idea what was causing him to go crazy with the barking like this. She kept trying to calm him down and comfort him, saying, "What's the matter? What's the matter?" and he kept facing that same spot on the ceiling and barking. About five minutes or so before I arrived (along with Debbie), just as suddenly, he stopped barking.

I was a little nervous to meet Ginger, since I had no idea why she was so intent on meeting me. But to be honest, I fell in love with her the moment I met her. She told me how she'd kept having this strong feeling that she needed to do this chart for me. We played with Nino a bit (I love dogs), and Ginger put him through his little routine of tricks he could do. Then we settled down to focus on my chart—I'd given Debbie my birth information in advance of our date. In the middle of this conversation, as Ginger was going over my chart and explaining everything, I had to stop her. I said, "I'm sorry to interrupt, but right next to you, in that corner, is a woman," and I went on to describe the woman to Ginger. It was her mother, who had crossed just a couple months before. (Her father, actually, too, had crossed; they'd died within a few weeks of each other.) Ginger was trying like crazy to hold it together because in her mind, she'd invited me there just to give me the information in my chart—as a gift. But I told her, "Your mother is standing right there and she's telling me about the house you were born in," and I went on to tell Ginger what her mother was saying. There were beautiful memories there—the two-family house, the alleyway, the garage in the back. Ginger confirmed that this described her home to a T and was certainly convinced this was indeed her mother visiting. And of course Nino Giuseppe had already announced her mother's presence even before I arrived.

Ginger had invited me purely to give me the gift of a reading, making a connection the Other Side had been urging her toward. As it turned out, I was able to reciprocate by bringing her messages from her mother. This was the auspicious beginning of one of the deepest, most rewarding friendships of my life.

Remember always to approach others with an open heart and be careful of making snap judgments—one never knows when one may be entertaining an angel unawares.

My friend Madeline first came to me as a client in 1999. She is probably one of the most beautiful women I have ever met in person. She always enjoyed my work and I always enjoyed looking at her. Her energy was amazing. I usually don't make friends with clients outside of my work. I have a very busy life, so I don't usually look for that. Plus, Concetta the medium and Concetta the person might seem different when someone gets to know me.

John and I had a couple we got along with really well—we'd always go out together, travel, hang out. They were so much fun; we laughed a lot, always agreed on where to go, and so much more. But when our friends adopted two daughters they became an "at home" couple with two small children. I was happy for them but sad at the same time. They weren't able to travel with us anymore and their focus, obviously, was the kids. I was so lonely for my girlfriend. I missed her laughter. I missed the friendship we'd all shared; I thought, "That's it, we'll travel by ourselves now."

But one night John and I were at Top of the Park restaurant in Boonton, New Jersey, and there were Mad and Steve. As the Other Side would have it, there was a long wait for a table, and Madeline jumped up and said, "Sit with us!" Well, long story short, Steve and John turned out to be two peas in a pod. Even when they're grumpy they're alike. And Madeline is a dream girl—sweet, kind, with a wonderful sense of humor, and she generously gives from her heart. She and Steve wanted us as friends; they liked us and we liked them. Almost ten years later, we are family. We got so lucky meeting them (thanks to the Other Side!). I love them more than I can ever say. Madeline has talents that I don't have. I feel bad sometimes because I know I call on her talents way more than she ever calls on mine. People always think that if you're a friend of mine I walk around doing readings for you all the time, which could not be farther from the truth. My friends know all my imperfections and love me anyway, thank God.

Lasting Relationships

When I do one of my big shows I make every effort to read as many people as possible. I know that's what they come for and I truly want to give comfort to those who come seeking that. Sometimes it's possible to both comfort people and have some fun at the same time.

At one of my shows a couple years ago, there was this whole contingent of folks, fifteen people, who had come together and took up two rows in the audience. By the break I hadn't gotten to that side of the room yet so a woman who was part of this group approached Ginger (who now does the introductions for the show so everyone knows she's part of the team). She introduced herself as the mother of the soul they were all there to hear from, a nineteen-year-old boy, Eric, who had died of brain cancer. With her were his former girlfriend, his sister, a couple aunts, and easily eight or nine friends—all lined up, young guys, handsome guys. The mother said, "Please tell Concetta this is my third time being here and I prayed so hard that we would get picked for a reading. That's why I brought all my son's friends, thinking the energy would be stronger in a group, that she could not miss it." Ginger relayed the message to me and I made sure to get over to them. Easily hearing the boy's spirit, I approached one of the friends and said, "Were you like his bodyguard?" He said, "Well, yeah. I was known to be his wingman. We watched out for each other." I told him, "Eric's pointing at you and saying, 'Thank you.'" Then I asked, "Who's 'D'? David? Danny?" (Besides Ginger speaking to me, Eric's spirit had actually stopped me in the hall during the break and told me to "Go find 'D' and tell him thank you for being more than a friend, like a brother.") The young man identified himself and I said, "Eric's saying the word 'bro' and that you knew each other since you were kids, that you had gone to school together all the way from first grade." This was confirmed. Then Eric told me that the wingman and another of his friends had been out together Friday night, the night before the show. I asked them, "Excuse me for asking this, but were you guys drinking?" They confirmed this and told me they'd been toasting Eric. I said, "He wants me to tell you, 'The push you felt was me.'" Both of them turned white. They told me that the night before they had been out drinking, they were across the room from each other and both felt someone push them in the back; they turned and looked at each other strangely, each knowing it couldn't have been the other one who pushed him because they were too far apart. Then I smelled pot. I said, "I know that you aren't drug addicts, but I smell this. Eric told me it was just for fun, nothing serious." The whole group, and the rest of the audience, laughed. This is one of my favorite things—being able to bring a message that will let everyone know that the soul is still with them, still enjoying them, that the spirit of their friendship goes on.

The souls really do what they can to let us know that. My friend Stephanie's very best friend had died of cancer when they were in their twenties. I was doing a reading for her when I first met her and didn't know her very well. I told her that she had a girlfriend standing there. I told her I kept hearing a song by Simon and Garfunkel, "Bridge over Troubled Water." The words are "If you need a friend, I'm sailing right behind, like a bridge over troubled water." She told me that any time she heard this song, she secretly always thought it was being played for her by this best friend who had passed away. And there it was. Confirmation. I still remember how good that made her feel, knowing her intuition had been right, that her friend was still around her.

Lovers and Soul Mates

Something I feel I need to clarify over and over because there is such a misconception about it is that our soul mate is not necessarily someone we will meet, fall in love with (perhaps dramatically), and marry. We might. But that's not what this special relationship is about. Our soul mate in this lifetime could be playing any role at all connected with us. They might be playing our father or mother, a sibling, a friend. Through all our lifetimes we'll be connected as if by an invisible thread. But we may not end up together every time. To confuse matters, there are others, besides our soul mate, with whom we'll feel a strong connection, and it's only over time that we can see that while intense, the connection was not deep or lasting.

For example, if we have been lovers in a previous lifetime and meet again in this lifetime we will have a strong energy connecting us. A girlfriend of mine told me the story of how when she was in her early twenties she was working in a combination pizza joint/

bar. She'd just taken orders from her various tables and was heading back to the bar to fill them, but when she got about twenty or so feet from the bar her eye was caught by a guy who was looking straight at her. In that instant, both their faces lit up with a magical kind of recognition. As she got nearer, without any sort of preamble or introduction, he said to her, "What time do you get off work?" She told him she got off at two A.M. and he said, "I'd like to take you to breakfast." (There was a twenty-four-hour Denny's nearby where young people often went after a night out.) They ended up living together for two years. This was not intended to be a life match for either of them, and she does not even feel he was her true soul mate. But the connection was undeniable and so strong that it's unlikely that it did not have karmic roots.

My husband, John, is the love of my life. Our relationship took work, but we've got a good solid thing going. We love our home, our kids, our friends. We have lots of fun together, love traveling together. I love him to death and wouldn't trade him, and I hope he wouldn't trade me. But our relationship might best be described by the definition of marriage in the Quaker religion. Quakers believe that a couple should marry in order to do God's work in the world, not necessarily to have children, though mutual love would be expected. Quakers were among the first, as a group, to approve of gay marriage because they said it wasn't important that a gay couple couldn't procreate so long as they were what Quakers call "helpmeets" (helpful to one another) in their life's work.

But Mushy is my soul mate. To this day I remember watching her in the school yard during recess, thinking she looked so sweet, laughing all the time. Even with other girls telling me that Mushy didn't like me, somehow I knew. It was a combination of a deep "knowing" I had and the Other Side reminding me that she was my soul mate. Our soul mate can be our lover, but this is not so common. More often it's someone looking out for you in another role.

> My name is Amy. I'm 25 years old. I just read your book "Do Dead People Watch You Shower." You rock my socks! I look at life at a different angle now. It put my mind at ease about a lot of things. I'm happier, more outgoing (just a little more), I listen and look for the small things.
>
> I just lost my sis~n~law of 15 years to cystic fibrosis. She was my sister, my rock, my angel, my best friend. Words can't describe that when she walked in a room how the room would light up b/c of her smile. She had this glow to her that only God could give. No matter how much pain she was in she smiled, laughed, cheered you up. She was the strongest person I knew in all of my years on this earth. I told her things that I know she took to her grave. I miss all of that. I think and hope she was my soul mate.
>
> I love you! I love what u do!

As I said in my first book, we may not be in an exclusive relationship with our soul mate in this lifetime. We may not even meet up with our soul mate in this lifetime if, for example, either we or our soul mate has other spiritual business to attend to somewhere else. But the connection we have with our soul mate has the same strength, substance, solidity, and spirit as the best marriages, and I do believe that we've been (or will be) married to our soul mate in other lifetimes, if not this one. What I don't think I was clear about earlier is that I have come to believe—perhaps controversially— that we may have more than one soul mate. This gift God gives us, that of our very being, is so spectacular and grand, I can't see it being limited in this way. "Sorry, ma'am. One soul mate per customer." I feel very blessed to have more than one soul mate—Mushy, my friend Madeline (Steve may well be one of John's soul mates), and others.

I may be sounding like a broken record, but we are all connected, we all need one another, and we never lose one another. In the flesh we can give each other a shoulder to cry on or share a laugh. In spirit our loved ones still provide us with comfort and try to make our lives better in any way they can. They are with us and will be with us, on this side and the Other Side, from one lifetime to the next.

A girl came to see me for a reading, the widow of a fireman who died in New York City. He came through wearing a fireman's hat and told me she was married again, which she confirmed. They'd had a seven-year marriage, and she had been devastated by his death but was completely convinced that it was he who had found somebody new for her and arranged for them to meet. She was happy now but told me she could never forget the love she felt for this man, her first husband, who was the great love of her life. During all this I said to her, "What is he trying to tell me? Did he speak a different language?" She said no, he didn't. I said, "Well, I'm hearing something that sounds like he speaks a different language. I'm hearing something that sounds like 'something-vee.' What could it be? 'Something-vee'?" And she said, "Oh my God." She told me that when she met him she had been working at a French bakery. That's how they met—when he came into the bakery. And sort of kidding, but really meaning it, he always called her *"mon vie,"* which means "my life" in French. Neither of them spoke French.

Not fluently or any other way, which is likely why he'd said *"mon"* instead *"ma."* But throughout their relationship, they would sign birthday cards and anniversary cards *"mon vie,"* "my life." And she said that at the funeral service she had given the eulogy, and at the end she'd said, "Rest in peace, *mon vie."* Even some present had not understood what she was saying and later had asked her to translate. She was blown away by that. I was, too!

That story is one of my favorites; it's such a touching love story and I'm a real sucker for love.

Not every story is as sweet . . .

One night not long ago, I went to visit Mushy in astro-travel (every now and again I will relax and allow my spirit to leave my body for these brief trips). She woke up while I was there and saw me peeking at her through her bedroom doorway. We talked about it later. She told me I'd said, "Mush?" and she'd said, "Concetta, get back on your broom and go home!" That's my soul mate!

Both our families and our friends (and others we encounter here) are from our Soul Link Group. We choose our families while we're on the Other Side and there are real reasons why we choose the souls and circumstances that we do. There honestly is wisdom in our choices, whether it seems like that once we're here or not. Our friends we choose on this side—sometimes to help us cope with our families! True friendship is a gift and a blessing. Real friends are there through the bitter and the sweet.

Reminders and Practices

- Consider your closest relationships. Think about what they mean to you, what you may be learning from each.

- To have a friend you need to be a friend. Is there some-one you can think of to whom you'd like to extend your friendship?

- Sit quietly with your eyes closed and breathe in deeply. As you breathe in, visualize your family and friends all being drawn in, close to your heart. Then, as you exhale, visual-ize this gathered energy and love going out through your entire Soul Link Group, and beyond that, from your Soul Link Group to all other Soul Link Groups in the world.

- Ask the Other Side to bring a new friend into your life.

8

Holidays Suck

Anyone who knows me knows that I like to shop as much as the next person. I love everything from major malls with their big anchor stores (Macy's, Bloomie's, Neiman Marcus) to street fairs, boutiques, garage sales, flea markets, and estate sales. And it's not just all about me, either. I get a charge from giving little gifts to friends and family—it could be for a birthday, to say thank you for something, or maybe just because I saw something and it made me think of a particular person and I knew they'd like it. Doesn't matter. It's fun. But I don't necessarily like there to be a particular date when it's mandated that I have to race around like a nut and find something—*anything*—for every single person I know or risk feeling lousy because I'm afraid someone might think I don't care about them. That's just *one* of the problems with holidays, at least the way we approach them these days, and I don't think I'm alone in the extra stress I often feel on some of these "special" days.

Because of their "specialness" holidays have an extra focus put on them; we have big expectations for them, whether it's a religious thing or a family thing or a combination of both. There's special food; we dress up fancy; there may be parties or extra events surrounding the holiday; we gather together with the people who matter to us. And we can put birthdays into this category, too, because I'm really talking about days in the year when something more is expected and if the day isn't a bit bigger, or a lot bigger, with everyone there who we want to be there, we feel bad or sad, or like we've let everyone down (which totally sucks, even if we don't have three ghosts showing up like Scrooge did to tell us all the ways we messed up) or everyone has let *us* down. The very fact that a particular day is a holiday, with high expectations programmed into us, just makes everything that we think is wrong in our lives seem ten times worse. Like, it's not enough that my boyfriend just dumped me, but it also has to be *Valentine's Day!* Bad enough I just got fired, but . . . on my *birthday?* The traffic to the beach was already awful *before* the car radiator boiled over. By the time we get there we won't find a parking space, the hot dogs will be all gone, the ice cream will be melted, and we'll miss the fireworks! I think in most families the parents do try to make holidays special for the kids but when we get older it's all on us to make these days special and to make everyone happy, starting with ourselves. Not always easy (see the last chapter on family).

When I first married John, his mother had already long established their holiday program and wasn't looking for any input from me as to what would make these occasions more enjoyable. She laid it all out for me: Christmas Eve, we do this; Christmas Day, it's that; on Easter, this is what we cook and here's when we eat. If she wanted an opinion (rare in itself) it was John she'd ask; anything I had to contribute was rejected. I spent ten years just showing up and trying to fit in, but even that was too much for her and the rest of his family. We were supposed to exchange gifts at Christmas and I always tried to get something the other person would really like. John always received lovely, personal presents; I, on the other hand, could look forward to a scented candle—something you might give a neighbor who had shown up unexpectedly and whom you were trying to make feel welcome by giving them something to unwrap with the family. It really sucked.

Increasingly, these occasions were so stressful for me that I'm not sure I could have stayed married, except for reassurances I was receiving from a few secret allies. The first was my deceased father-in-law, who apparently was making my marriage his project. He had some regrets about how he had been when he was living and I think he was now trying to be as helpful to his son as possible. In any case, he began showing up the first year I was with John and always was encouraging to me, telling me that things were going to get better (hard for me to believe, I'll admit) and that he—unlike other members of the family—was glad I was with his son. At the time I could never tell John that his father, in spirit, was consoling me. I wasn't "out" yet as a medium, even to my husband, and I'm afraid that would just have given his mother's case against me more substance. The second was my own dear mother, who kept assuring me that life was long and things would change. I had little income in those days and nowhere to go other than back to my parents' home, and I still loved my husband, so I decided to trust his dead father and my living mother and stick it out.

It took me a long while, however, to understand that things wouldn't just change on their own, that it was up to me. Finally, a few of my guardian angels, along with John's father, began to show me images of holidays as they would be in my future—nothing at all like the grim events I'd gotten used to, but truly joyful occasions. Since I have full confidence in the Other Side, these little "slide shows" were just the kick in the pants I needed. Seeing what was possible made me determined to make some changes. It made me understand that it was up to me to pull myself out of that situation—leave the drama behind—and create my own joy with my own family and friends.

Happy Is Up to Us

Making ourselves happy can seem a tall order if we have lost a loved one. The loss is so keenly felt at these special times when what seems most important is being among those we care about, having them share the day, the songs and celebrations, the cake and Manischewitz, the cookies and champagne, the ham or the turkey. I have my own personal experience with how hard this can be, and I'll tell you the story.

Thanksgiving Day 2008, I was really looking forward to our annual get-together at my best friend Mushy's house. The usual crowd would be in attendance—Mushy; her husband, Bob; their daughter and son-in-law Jennifer and Peter and their three kids; my brother Bobby, his wife, Choi, and their daughter (my niece and namesake), Bobbie Concetta; Uncle Gerry (my mother's brother); and John, my mother, and me. As usual, Mushy had been preparing for days, and for anyone who knows Mushy's cooking, the thought of that alone is enough to make your mouth water! She makes the most amazing sweet potatoes and her garlic soup is to die for. But the next morning, Thanksgiving Day, I got a call from Bobby, who told me that around four in the morning my mother had gotten sick and was having severe stomach pains and that she'd been taken to the hospital. That did not sound too good, but I wasn't led to believe that anyone thought the situation was life threatening. She'd had a few small health issues in recent years and had always been fine in the end, so I was just sorry she'd miss the party. Knowing she would be a little upset not to spend the day together with all of us, I planned to have dinner with everyone and then head to the hospital to visit her. I thought maybe I could even bring her a bite of something good that she'd enjoy. She'd definitely be missed, along with Bobby, Choi, and my niece, who were staying with Mommy at the hospital.

Thanksgiving morning, John and I had to go rescue Uncle Gerry and guide him in—he'd gotten turned around somehow on his way to Mushy's—but that was the only mishap before we sat down to dinner. Still, the day was definitely a downer. I felt bad for Mushy, who had gone to a lot of trouble for our annual party. She'd cooked up a storm and there was too much food and too few people to eat it. Also I'd gotten a few calls from Choi at the hospital that did not sound at all upbeat regarding my mother's condition, so all day I was torn between not wanting to be yet another guest to bail on Mushy and feeling like I really should be at the hospital. Finally, around three thirty, I said to Mush, "I'm so sorry, but I really have to get over to the hospital, I really need to go see Mommy." Of course she understood, but the party was pretty well ruined when John and I left in one car with Uncle Gerry following behind us in his. As we approached our exit, my cell phone rang. It was my brother Bobby saying, "Con. Mom's gone." *Gone?* We turned around and drove home, in shock.

How was this possible? I had spoken to my mother just the day before and she was completely fine! Our conversation had been totally ordinary—"How are you, fine, we'll see you tomorrow for dinner, I love you, good-bye." I had the TV on and Judge Judy was giving her verdict, so to be honest, I was hardly even paying attention to the phone conversation. I could not believe that was the last time I would hear my mother's voice in this life.

When I got in the house, all I could think was, "I want to hear her voice." I have a junk drawer that I just throw stuff into, including, sometimes, tapes from my answering machine. Sometimes there's a funny message or something I want to remember, and I knew that I had a few that had my mother's voice on them. I never mark the tapes so I figured it would take me a few tries to find one of those. I pulled out the first one I grabbed and put it in the machine, then without even rewinding I pressed "play." Immediately I heard, "Hi, kids. It's Mommy. I just wanted to say happy Thanksgiving. I love you kids very much." Without even knowing, I had grabbed a tape from exactly a year ago with exactly the message I needed to hear. When we received a copy of Mommy's certificate of death, the time was 4:54 P.M., exactly twenty-four hours from when she and I had last spoken.

As terrible as my Thanksgiving was that year, I couldn't help but think of another Thanksgiving my mother had told me about that she had experienced in her childhood. That one was the very definition of a holiday that sucked.

As I mentioned earlier, my mother and her brothers, Gerry, John, and Daniel, grew up in an orphanage where they were treated very badly. They had been taken away from their mother, who was an alcoholic, too young and messed up ever to have had kids, but she had them and then had them taken away. Only occasionally did she visit my mother and uncles, but when my mother was seven years old, a little before the holiday her mother told them that she'd come get them Thanksgiving Day and take them home to dinner. She hadn't said when she'd pick them up, but on the day, my mother and her brothers got dressed early and went to wait for their mother by the front gate of the orphanage, eager for this time together. They waited for her there all day long and knowing how November in New Jersey usually is they were likely chilled to the bone. At around dusk, a nun came out and took them by the hands. "Kids, come back inside," she said brusquely. "Your mother's not coming. She's dead."

Her mother had been only twenty-seven. I can't even imagine a child being told in this way that their mother was gone forever. But now I saw it: Seventy years ago, my mother's mother had promised to come for her on Thanksgiving, and now she had done exactly that. She'd come for my mother, on Thanksgiving Day, to take her home.

I remember my mother telling me how she had gone to her mother's funeral and had thought she looked so beautiful wearing a pink chiffon dress. She described her as "perfect" and "beautiful." It was after my father passed away in 2001 that she asked us kids to meet her at Brown's Funeral Parlor in Nutley, New Jersey. She told us that she did not want us to be stressed when she eventually crossed as well. She told us about her insurance policy and exactly what she wanted. While we all sat there, she had everything drawn up and written down. She didn't want anything fancy. She told us, "If they'd have had a pine box, I'd have taken it." And she warned us: "Don't change *anything*. I don't want you kids to spend another dime on anything." She sat there laughing at us, joking, making all her own arrangements. The guy who was helping us out would say, "Okay, Eleanor. What else do you want? What kind of flowers, what kind of music?" And each time he'd suggest an "extra," she'd reply, "No, no thank you. I don't need that." But she said that she'd like to be buried like her mother in a pink chiffon dress.

It took me a long time to recover from the shock of my mother's sudden passing. To be honest, I lost it and was not much help to anyone. I don't know what we would have done without Choi, who took upon herself the chore of going to the senior residence where Mommy had lived and packing up seventy-seven years of my mother's life. And somehow, somewhere, she even found a pink chiffon dress so my mother could be buried in it just as she'd requested. I'm so grateful for my sister-in-law stepping in and handling everything. Honestly, if it had been left up to me, I don't think I could have gotten it done. I was completely devastated.

Obviously, there will never be another Thanksgiving Day when I don't think of my mother. And how can I not feel both sadness and guilt? Like, I'm a *psychic medium*, for goodness' sake! How could I not have known? And how could I, as a loving daughter, not have been paying attention when I last spoke with her? Why did I stay at the party, having a meal, instead of being by my mother's side at the hospital? The Other Side has told me often enough, and I know from other instances in my life, that having this ability in no way protects me from the human experience. I feel the same losses and hurts, the same regrets and sorrows, as any other person. Each of us has our own particular lessons in any given lifetime, but for the most part I'm on the same human journey as you.

But what is the lesson here? When we are missing someone we love, how can we not give in to melancholy on an ordinary day, let alone a day when every expectation is that our life should look like a Hallmark card? Where are our parents and grandparents? Where is our partner, where are our kids? Where are the perfect decorations and the amazing spread of food? Isn't it normal to feel sad or depressed if we are far from home, don't have children, can't afford a splashy party, have lost one of our dearest ones? What does the Other Side have to say about that?

Here's the deal: Whatever else is intended for us in this lifetime, we are meant to be happy. Happy is up to us. We are meant to *find* happiness or *make* happiness, even when our circumstances are imperfect. Even when circumstances suck.

The Wall of Grief

I think the worst thing of all with the holidays is not having with you the people you care about. As I mentioned, our usual Thanksgiving Day party was already a bust just from our family members being missing. I'd like to think that if we'd known that everyone was well and happy, just not able to make it that day, we'd have had a nice celebration, maybe wishing they were there but also enjoying our nice, if smaller, gathering and Mushy's good cooking. It was the absence plus the worry that put the real damper on things, and of course that was before I knew how much worse it would get. Now my mother would never be with us again. And I know that is a pain that so many face on a special day—an absence that is final. That's unbelievably hard to deal with. *But is it the reality?*

No, it's not. And I can totally promise you this: Our loved ones never truly leave us. They are with us forever, all the time. But grief can create a wall that makes it more difficult for them to reach us.

As I've already mentioned, when my mother crossed, just like anyone else who loses a dear family member, I was devastated. Emotionally, yes. But even more, I completely lost the ability to hear the Other Side. This silence, this disconnection from the wisdom that had guided me my whole life, scared me to death. I always say that I'm not "gifted" so much as I have an ability. But when I lost my ability it made me recognize that even if I don't like the term "gifted" because it sounds like I'm full of myself, my ability really is a gift. I couldn't believe it had been taken away, leaving me doubly bereft. It wasn't like someone who has the ability to paint but when a loved one died was sad and just didn't have the heart to paint for a while. I literally was *unable* to hear the spirits talk. It was like the Other Side was saying, "No, you don't get anything special here. You get to feel this loss just like anyone else would feel it." And I did. It hurt so bad. I was like a crazy person, literally walking into walls. Even though John tried hard to console me, I truly felt alone. For a time, I believed maybe we *are* alone.

In my own grief, I was deep in a place of blocked consciousness. My lifelong knowledge of the Other Side told me that my mother was not gone, that she was in spirit and still "here" even though she had crossed. I felt sure she wanted to communicate with me, let me know she was home, safe and happy. But the heavy emotions that had hold of me formed an impenetrable wall that even a spirit could not reach me through. This compounded my emotional state because it made me feel like a phony. Also, I was terribly tired but so stressed that I could not sleep except fitfully. The great irony was that once my body and soul were so exhausted I couldn't stay awake anymore and I finally did sleep fully, my unconscious was able to take over and that's when I began to recover. As my conscious mind drifted away, carrying the heaviness with it, my subconscious was able to relax and listen and finally hear from my mother (which I'll say more about later).

This was a big lesson for me. Just like anyone, I have lessons to learn and sometimes I even need to relearn the lessons I've been teaching. It came home to me with the very first client I had once I resumed my business.

Unseen, but Here
This client and her sister had been extremely close, but her sister had suddenly died in November. Needless to say, my client was

feeling the loss, but she seemed to be coping surprisingly well. It turned out she'd discovered the secret for herself. During the reading I said to her, "What is it about a fan? Something about a fan—your sister is telling me." The woman smiled and shared with me that after her sister's funeral she had come back home, feeling very lost and alone. She had gone directly to her bedroom and lay down. The day was chilly so the windows were closed, yet as she lay there looking up, the blades of her ceiling fan began to spin around, then stopped. Hopefully, she said aloud, "Donna, if that's you, make the ceiling fan do it again." The blades—seemingly on their own—made another full rotation. Her hope and willingness to trust in the possibility of her sister's presence allowed her to have this connection. "I know my sister has not really left me," she confided. And she is absolutely right.

A few years ago I threw a party in my home for my friend Ginger's sixtieth birthday. Some of the guests I hadn't met before—Mushy was there, and Ginger's partner Wendy, and our friend Sue, but many of the guests were friends of Ginger's whom I didn't know—but that didn't stop us girls from all having a wonderful time. I have to say I have a pretty nice home—John built it and it's truly beautiful. The rooms are large so we can do the entertaining we both love. We were spread out in bunches here and there, eating, drinking, talking, laughing. Gifts for Ginger were piled up in the living room and ten P.M. was the designated time for unwrapping her presents. At a little before ten we started calling everyone into the living room with Ginger settled on the sofa and her packages in front of her. But just as it turned ten o'clock, all the lights in the living room went out! But we could see that in other parts of the house—the dining room, the kitchen, and so forth—the lights were still on. Only in the living room was it dark. You can imagine the scene, a whole room full of women, not scared, but it was a little spooky so we were just wondering, "What on *earth!*" And of course making various joking comments and at the same time trying to figure it out. Mushy, all business, immediately said, "Where's your fuse box?" and started across the room to see if maybe a fuse had blown that controlled just that room, but at the same moment Ginger looked at me and said, "Concetta, who is it?" After just a second of concentration I said, "Oh my God, Ginger, it's your parents! They want to wish you a happy birthday!" And then, as if satisfied that the message had been understood, just as quickly as the lights had gone out, they came back on. Mushy had just gotten to the fuse box and stood frozen there as the lights came on. She looked at all of us and said, "I didn't even *touch* it yet." The look on her face, along with the broken tension, sent all of us giggling again and Sue couldn't resist a quip: "It's ten o'clock. Do you know where your parents are?" Which of course cracked us all up. For Ginger, I'm sure there was not another present she received that night that meant more to her than her parents showing up in spirit to wish her a happy sixtieth birthday —that was the icing on the cake.

Reaching Out to Them

You don't have to wait for them to make contact. You can certainly reach out to loved ones who are absent.

At the end of the summer in 2010, John and I took a long trip driving around Ireland. We'd never been there before and it had long been on my list of places to go since my family on my mother's side comes from there. I met a woman who told me that every Christmas her family goes to the grave site of her deceased mom and tells her all the news of the holiday season. She told me that the past year she'd made her usual trip, and after Christmas was over she had a dream of her mother telling her she was happy in the light and saying thank you for her Christmas gift. Her mom knew she had brought a cousin with her to the grave site who had not been able to make it to her mother's funeral. She mentioned the flowers they'd put on the grave—a particular kind, she told me, but at the moment the name is escaping me. She said the next day she woke up still feeling a warm glow left over from her dream. She asked me, "Is it true, did my mother really know we were there?" It never ceases to amaze me when I'm asked that. I said, "You know the answer better than me." She said, "You're right, I know she came to me."

Reminders and Practices

• Decide It's Up to You

If you're waiting for someone to come along and show you a good time, you may have a long wait. The advice from the Other Side is to take matters into your own hands. If your usual holiday is a downer, try celebrating with a different group of people with whom you feel a loving rapport. One of the best ways to make yourself happy is to try making others happy. Maybe you can't please He-or-She-Who-Will-Not-Be-Pleased. But try spending some quality time and attention on a cousin you adore but see only once a year, or a child or older person who may be bored or feeling left out. Ask them what *they* would like to do. Give them the gift of your full attention.

• Hold Your Traditions Lightly

Most of our holidays have a certain amount of tradition attached to them, whether religious or certain practices that have been done year to year within the family, to the point that we can't even think about the holiday without thinking of those activities. I'm not saying you should skip Mass or forget your fast if these are meaningful components of your holiday. But try not to be so rigid about "what's supposed to happen" on a given holiday that anything that goes contrary to that strikes you as a disappointment. If you're bursting into tears because someone forgot the pignoli cookies or you're one hard-boiled egg short for Passover, then, Houston, you've got a problem. Holding your traditions lightly does not mean letting them completely go but giving them room to breathe and not feeling crushed—or angered—either by things that don't go according to plan or by new innovations. If there are kids in your family, the likelihood is that at some point, however many years down the road, those kids will be bringing home a partner for the holidays and that person may come from a family with other traditions. Not only is it welcoming for you to be open to something that may make them feel more comfortable, there's also a chance that their suggestion might be something you enjoy and even come to cherish.

• **Send Holiday Greetings to Your Missing Loved Ones**
Don't wait around for your deceased parents to turn out the lights. If there is someone you are missing, take your own warm wishes to them. The surest way I know to make contact with our loved ones, whether you feel you are particularly psychic or not, is through relaxed meditation. In this state the conscious mind subsides and the subconscious comes forward and opens to realities we are usually not aware of.

If you are someone who has a little more trouble quieting yourself and concentrating, one way is to take file cards; write your hopes, dreams, prayers, and desires on them; and look at them like they were crib notes for a test. Using your "cue cards," invite your loved one to show herself. Try some of these: *Mom, I love you, I miss you, I need you to let me know you're here with us.* Or *I invite you to turn off a light or play a song I will know is from you.* Or *Could you have someone we both know and I haven't heard from in a while call me?* Or just simply, *Please show me something I will know is from you.* Also, try to hold this thought: *I am not afraid to see something that is a message from you.*

The thoughts and messages on your cards should be personal between you and your loved one. Don't hold back, but be reasonable. Don't ask them to set the table, ask them to sit at it.

Once you have "voiced" your messages, stay quiet and relaxed and just listen. Give it time; stay open. You may not hear a voice; it's more likely you will hear a response from a spirit as a thought. If at first you are not "hearing" a response, please do stay with it. Trust, believe, *know* that your loved one *is* there. Especially on the holidays—where families are gathered together and they can get the biggest bang for their spiritual buck—they love to be around us.

• Don't Forget the Scented Candle

You never know who may show up on a holiday—an extra friend who couldn't get home to their own family, a neighbor whom your spouse spontaneously invited, the exchange student staying with Uncle Joe and Aunt Sally. It's nice to have a little something already wrapped and tucked away somewhere handy that you can give that person to open when others are opening gifts. Making another person feel welcome in your home will give you a nice un-sucky holiday glow.

9

Mistakes, I've Made a Few...

It is possible for you to become so defiled in this world that your own mother and father will abandon you. If that happens, God will believe in your own ability to mend your own ways.

—Bob Dylan, Grammy Lifetime Achievement Award
acceptance speech

Heaven is perfection. Our world is full of errors and corrections. Think of it like a car with a finicky engine that stutters a bit until you run it awhile and then smooths out, or a baby making the transition to toddler—falling after every third step until they get steady on their legs. Here, none of us is a saint (and even a saint struggles with character flaws). Here, we have false starts; here, we make a lot of mistakes.

A year or so ago, I was going to an event in New York City. I'm used to driving in New Jersey, but in New York I don't know where I am or where anything else is and I can get a little crazy.

I hate being late—it's so disrespectful to whoever is waiting for you—but the irony is that when I got caught in traffic, which was completely out of my control and completely out of the driver's control, I started losing it. I was thinking about the people on the other end and how they'd be kept waiting and might think I didn't take our meeting seriously or didn't care. So I started getting wound up and giving pretty strident "suggestions" to the driver and to the other cars around us, completely forgetting myself. I was so afraid that the people I was meeting were going to think badly of me that I wasn't considering the people I was presently with or how I was treating them. The driver didn't deserve my comments—the situation wasn't his fault. He was already doing the best he could do—it's not like he *wanted* to be stuck in traffic. He'd certainly just as soon have gotten me where I was supposed to be so he could get me out of his car! He probably just wanted to be done with his day and back home with his family. The other cars around us were pretty much in the same situation we were: stuck. And I was giving no thought to the fact that in those cars were other human beings like myself who probably had places they were supposed to be.

I honestly believe most everyone lives their life making their best effort to do the right thing. So much of what we manage to screw up is just due to the extreme complexity and speed of our lives. Makes sense, doesn't it? If you are only dealing with yourself or a handful of people and a small number of tasks, there're just fewer opportunities to make mistakes. If you were a monk on a silent retreat, pretty much the only thing you could do wrong is open your mouth. But most of us have dozens of opportunities, seemingly every moment of the day, to not only open our mouths, but also to insert our foot!

So many of our errors result just from going too fast. We have so many expectations placed upon us, and we're accountable to numerous simultaneous competing demands. We need to care for our families, maintain our homes, manage a commute, and perform our jobs with competence and style, showing up well groomed with a big smile. In the age of e-mail, where the in-box fills to overflowing overnight, work alone is enough stress, let alone anything extracurricular—seeing friends, attending church, "doing" a holiday, planning an event or a vacation—and God help anyone who gets sick. This whole idea of "multitasking" is presented to us like it's the Holy Grail—like it's not enough to be human beings, we're supposed to be frickin' eight-armed octopuses doing sixteen things at once.

It's no wonder we find ourselves acting in haste or "not in our right minds" and making bad decisions. One bad decision may easily be followed by others, either because we simply lose control of a situation or because we're trying to fix something. If we're caught in the midst of this and are embarrassed by it, there can be the temptation to tell a fib to cover ourselves or try to deflect the blame onto someone else. The whole thing snowballs. Or another common scenario is that we get so overwhelmed we simply avoid the big to-do pile. It's just too much to face so we pretend it's not there, but before long it's not just too much to handle; it's actually crushing. Too often good, well-intentioned people are left feeling like they're disappointing themselves and others.

Tools to Keep Your Cool

Unfortunately, this is the reality on the physical plane in the twenty-first century. We all need to find both practical and spiritual ways to deal with it. Many people now are looking for ways to simplify their lives—and good luck with that. But there are two spiritual concepts I can recommend that can help us manage this load of you-know-what we all find ourselves in the middle of. One is borrowed from the Buddhists, the other from Jewish mysticism, the Kabbalah.

The first concept is "staying in the moment." Again, the pace of modern life has us constantly in our heads, spinning forward and backward—"What do I need to do?" "Where'd I put that thing?" The trick here is to slow down, or even stop for a moment, and give our full focus to the situation or task in front of us. This is called "mindful awareness" and it's not something you do once, it's something we need to practice until it becomes our second nature, our default way of operating. As a spiritual practice it can be a form of meditation, but it's a very useful tool just to get us through our day less carelessly. When we're focused on one thing at a time, giving a situation all due consideration, it's simply less likely we're going to make that first mistake (unintentionally hitting "send" on an e-mail to the wrong person; making a snap, end-justifies-the-means decision; losing our mind in traffic) that leads to others. This takes time and repeated effort to master—and it's something I personally am still working on—but it's well worth it.

The second concept is that in order to get the Light we must do what is difficult. In Kabbalistic terms, "the Light" refers to "God the Creator" and equals "all that is good." So in other words, in order to get anything that is good we must be willing to work for it. Our human inclination, very often and understandably, is to try to avoid discomfort. But in trying to avoid discomfort we frequently make mistakes that put us in real pain. And we certainly aren't rewarded for it. On the Other Side we are completely fulfilled and need nothing. On this side if there's something we want or need, we have to dig ditches for it. It's just that simple: The physical plane requires physical effort. So to me, this concept really amounts to, "Hold the complaints, hold your nose, put your head down, and push through it." Doesn't sound very spiritual, does it? But that's it. The pile isn't getting any smaller by your wishing it would. If you've got too much on your plate and you can figure out a way to lighten the load, then God bless you. If not, then it's yours to do.

One thing I've noticed is that nice people tend to let themselves get buried simply because they hate to tell anyone no. Knowing that my readers are all nice people, I'm going to suggest that you get more familiar with that word. Consider it a third maybe-not-so-spiritual concept that'll help you manage the load. You can't be everything to everyone; trying to be is definitely a recipe for dropping a ball or two and making mistakes or disappointing someone. In physical form we have limited time and limited energy and we need to learn to work within that reality.

Our Spiritual Guidance System

We make incidental errors every day, little stuff that gets us into hot water that we hopefully can correct without making our problem any worse. But sometimes we actually hurt somebody else, and that's a more serious problem.

When I was ten or eleven I used to babysit a lot for children in the neighborhood and one little girl was my favorite; I really loved her. But one time I remember being with her and some of the other girls on the block began making fun of her, and I went along with it. I didn't defend her. To the core of my soul I knew how wrong it was. I still hurt inside just thinking about it, because I knew then and now how wrong it was. It went beyond that moment, beyond those other girls. I remembered being in another time and place and it was me that someone was making fun of, and now I was taking part in hurting someone else. It was like a tug-of-war, this interior knowing and on the outside this pull to "go along with the group"—the mean girls who at that moment seemed stronger. Like it was more important to please them than to do what I knew was right. If I could ever go back in time for a do-over, I would go back and stop laughing and do something else, with love; that's what I'd want to go back for.

I do have recollections of being on the Other Side before coming here. I've always had a deep sense of familiarity when I hear the dead talking to me. Even before I could put it into words I had an understanding that this world that we see around us is not all there is. I always, even as a child, had an awareness of my own soul and knew, deep within, the difference between right and wrong. But I don't think this is because I'm psychic. We all have this GPS with God, our intuition and emotions that tell us even as an event is in motion if we are not doing what is right. It's where the spiritual meets the physical, and we feel it in our gut (we get queasy) or in our heart (we literally become heartsick). We might even actually hear the voice of our better angels warning us about our behavior. But if we're so caught up in the event that we don't notice all the signals, we certainly are aware of our wrongdoing afterward and feel the sting of regret. I think anyone who reaches adulthood very likely has a memory of something they did or didn't do that left them feeling ashamed.

I don't recommend holding on to negative feelings like guilt and shame, but it's important that we give them their due. Again, these emotions are part of a spiritual guidance system. When we do something nice for someone else, often we'll feel a warmth inside—a good feeling—and when we do something harmful to another person, we get an unpleasant feeling, reminding us that this is something we don't want to repeat and that a correction is in order. This unpleasant feeling holds us "in the moment" until we acknowledge our action and can find some way to begin to repair it.

Sorry!

While our mistakes often happen unconsciously, there is no correction that happens that way. Any act of atonement (look at the word: "at-one-ment"—it's bringing us back into alignment and connection with the other party) must be fully conscious and intentional. We have to choose to do the right thing. Then we have to do it.

Doing what is difficult is not always about taking on some strenuous, time-consuming task. Sometimes the difficult thing is as simple as saying "I'm sorry." And frankly, saying that we're sorry should be a little difficult. If it slips off our tongue too easily, it could be because it's our habit to be in a position where a "sorry" is necessary. If that's the case, we need to be giving more thought to our actions generally—we're supposed to be learning from our mistakes, not making them over and over again. And once you recognize that a true "I'm sorry" is in order, don't let ego and pride stand in the way, like Fonzie Fonzarelli on *Happy Days* struggling to get an apology out of his mouth, stammering, "I was wruh-wruh-wruh-wrong."

Ideally, we won't be doing too many things for which we need to seek forgiveness. But this is the real world, not the ideal. To err is all too human. We need to be willing to do the difficult, own up to our mistakes and extend a heartfelt "I'm sorry."

Hunting for Harmony

This side of the veil has a lot of misunderstanding, illusion, and delusion. Oftentimes we have to work hard to "get" what's going on or "get" another person—what's going on in their head. Sometimes we will struggle a lifetime to know someone in our own Soul Link Group, to understand what our relationship is and what the lessons between us are. Frequently it can seem like we're just different and we'll never see eye to eye. Like that person was just put on this planet to frustrate us. Many times others' behaviors or points of view that seem inexplicable to us are driven by their fears.

I remember a client who came to me a long time ago. The reading went wonderfully; his parents had come through and celebrated his being able to hear them. He was happy about this because he knew that in life they would not have approved of his going to a medium; he'd told me that. And during the reading, his parents confirmed that he knew they would have disapproved, but now they were so happy to say that they were great in the light of God. Also during the reading they said things I didn't understand, and they mentioned names he didn't validate. But about two months later he called my office and gave Elena a message for me. Apparently he was adopted, and all of his life he wondered about his birth parents. His adoptive parents did not ever want to help him find them or contact them. There was a lot of hurt and friction around this. So when his biological mother tried to meet him he turned her down. But during the reading they had mentioned her name and had encouraged him to reach out to her. Now that they were on the Other Side, their fear was gone. It was all about love, not selfishness or jealousy or fear of the unknown or that they would lose him. He never mentioned this to me during the reading. However the message was clear to him. He went on to say that he had gotten in touch with his mother and found out so many details of his birth and adoption. He told Elena that he wanted me to know that he has finally forgiven his biological mother and his adopted mother. He was finally at peace.

Whenever there is conflict, both parties think they are right. We have several possibilities here: 1) Both are wrong; 2) both are part right; 3) each is right relative to their own circumstances but not to the other's. Given that we know that this side of the veil is not perfection, even if we struggle to find harmony we may not succeed. But it's important to at least try to see the other's point of view. In conflict, no one is happy, so if you're in pain, the other person is as well. There are many different levels on which we can relate to someone and it doesn't further us spiritually to say, "Well, if we can't agree on this, then we can't agree on anything." Sometimes, on this side, the best thing we can do is agree to disagree about a particular subject and go on to enjoy one another in other areas with the knowledge that eventually we will know perfect understanding between ourselves and the other person.

Prayer
All that said, we don't want to wait to get to the Other Side before we have any sense of the peace that comes with understanding.

We are here to learn. But in order to have understanding on this plane we really have to want it. We have to desire it, and we have to set that desire in motion as an *intention* with *energy* behind it. The best way I know to do this is by dialing the 800 number to the Holy Spirit: *prayer.*

Like any other human being I have my issues that can sometimes blind me to another person's truth. I find myself in the middle of situations that seem crazy or messed up and I always want to do that human thing of trying to figure out who's right and who's wrong, who's to blame—it's just the way my mind works. I'm also wanting to figure out if I did the right thing in a given circumstance or whether I owe someone an apology. The bottom line is that I want peace in my life, and even if I'm able to let go of other people's behavior toward me, I don't feel peaceful when I have questions about my own behavior. I worry about that, and I also really do want understanding of the other person, why they feel the way they do about something. All this yearning for understanding can be brought directly to the Other Side in your prayers.

As I've already mentioned, my mother had a horrible childhood. She was put in a terrible institution that was run by people who said they represented God. And they allowed her to be beaten, made fun of, raped, and denied food and medical treatment. She always said to me, "That was not God; I don't hold it against God." I knew about this as a young person and I had a very hard time with it. I was so angry, knowing what was done to her and that it was done by people who wore the clothes of God and collars of priests. I couldn't understand this, and to tell the truth I still can't. But she used to say to me all the time that was not God and they were not representatives of God. They looked like it—

they certainly told the world they represented God. But the truth is, they didn't. My mother had a peace within herself, sure in that truth. It took me a long time even to *want* to understand. It was her example that finally brought me to that point. And it still took a lot of prayer, saying, "God, take this over from me, I want to be at peace. This is not feeling good to me. I don't understand. Please help me. I want to be at peace." Many times simply handing over our lack of understanding can alleviate the pain and frustration of not understanding. But keep your eyes and mind open, too, for situations that may show up—as if played out for you, and possibly involving total strangers—that give you some insight into your own situation.

No Excuses—Get the Lesson

The energy of the Other Side is all about answers and solutions, a state of perfection. Here, we have a lot of questions, problems. You have to remember, as I said before, that we're all being irritated, but the irritation hopefully ends up producing a pearl or polishing up a beautiful diamond. The things that bother us should challenge us to improve ourselves—our own behavior and our understanding. Peace and harmony are things we're looking for all the time, to become one with God in a perfect state of harmony. So how do we go about that? Do you put your focus and attention on the problem or on the solution? Of course it's better to put our attention on the solution, but that's where we all get hung up.

When kids make a mistake, instead of simply working on a correction, they're very often looking to find a reason, something that will explain or excuse their incorrect behavior or their failure to do the right thing. Kids can always come up with a good reason why something happened—she did this, or he said that, or they made this happen so I can't do this. They're so creative! They've got all kinds of reasons. Hopefully by the time we've been around the block a few times we realize that if we focus on the problem—or focus on our reasons for the problem—we get more problems. In order to make a correction or find solutions we need to focus on the solution, not on evading blame by creating explanations of the circumstances that created the problem. The explanations are a waste of energy and at the end of the day they don't change or solve anything. Kids have plenty of energy, but as we get older and don't have quite as much we're better off saving ours for working on solutions instead of the spin.

In order to be proactive about getting the lesson, we can check in with our spiritual guidance system, or emotions. What are we feeling? Are we feeling ashamed about something we did? Do we feel anger or hurt? What are these emotions telling us? It's important to examine these feelings. Holding on to unexamined feelings simply creates suffering. But we have these for a reason. Feeling shame or guilt tells us that we've committed an injury that we need to correct if we can, offer an apology for, seek atonement for. Feeling anger may mean we've experienced or witnessed an injustice of some kind. Is there something we can do to change the circumstances that create the injustice? Hurt can signal some kind of misunderstanding. Is there any way we can improve the communication, explain the situation, find common ground?

Once you've explored what you are feeling and taken what actions you can toward resolution, letting go of these emotions is a gift you give yourself. Letting go of anger can be like letting go of a toothache! If negative emotions are lingering, we can ask ourselves, "What is it doing for me? Why am I holding on to this? What is it teaching me?" Then ask, "Do I want peace? Can I realize and accept that I don't always have to be right? Am I a victim? Do I want to be a victim?"

We can also use prayer to help us move past these emotions and tell God that we want to turn them over. Say, "I'll let you take care of these for me. I want to be at peace." I often do that, and then I'll go on, I'll wash a dish, make a cup of tea, vacuum, find some distraction, and let God do his healing thing, easing and erasing the pain.

The more you exercise your prayer muscle the stronger it gets. When I'm struggling with a lesson, I may simply say a prayer and then go about my day, working around my house or shopping. In a sense, I'm doing "nothingness" but God is at work. I feel better that I gave my issues over to the big guns in town. The Holy Spirit is in all of us on this earth—just waiting for us to ask for help. Once you trust that, and do that, you'll suddenly see a solution you didn't see before. You'll go, "Oooh, there it is!" It's a question of giving it over wholeheartedly, then patiently waiting for the insight, inspiration, and peace to come. If you don't ask for God's help you aren't taking advantage of the very beautiful and powerful assistance that is there for all of us.

Peace, Not Punishment

Everyone here is on a different part of his or her journey; not all souls are evolved to the same degree. Depending on what they are here to learn a soul may have selected parents who are not going to be great role models. They may have selected very difficult circumstances for this life's lessons, or it may simply be their turn in this lifetime to experience being the one who causes another harm, to learn what it feels like on that side of the equation. So there are definitely souls who commit acts for which "I'm sorry" just isn't going to cut it on this side. If you do something that harms others, society is going to take a chunk out of your butt, maybe give you a "time out" to consider the harm you've done. Depending on the act or acts you've committed, it may be for a few days or it may be the rest of your physical existence. But even those who have committed serious wrongs—so long as they have not willfully taken another life—will get a fresh start when they cross.

I'm often asked about payback on the Other Side—like if someone hasn't done the right thing when they are here, or has been mean or cruel to others. People want to know what's going to happen to them, or they want to assure themselves that someone who's treated them badly will get their just desserts. Well, the answer is that God isn't in the business of punishing us. God is pure love and goodness. He doesn't punish us; we punish ourselves. When we cross to the Other Side, if we've done things we are ashamed of, if we've harmed someone or been unfair or made people unhappy, we will experience full understanding of how bad that really is. We won't be able to kid ourselves anymore about how "all's fair in love and war" or "they had it coming" or anything like that. We'll see so clearly how wrong we were and we will want to make amends. Many, many times when I'm doing a reading I'll hear from a soul who has treated another person badly and they'll be saying over and over how sorry they are. And the truth is, if someone who has seriously wronged you has already crossed, they are more likely to be knocking themselves out to assist you here in any way they can. Don't be surprised if something good comes your way that has their fingerprints, so to speak, all over it.

Another concern I hear in my work—over and over—is that people think that someone over there is mad at them. Maybe *we're* the one who wronged someone. Or in the midst of really difficult decisions we have to make about a loved one's health crisis or about their former possessions after they have crossed, we're worried we made a wrong decision, didn't do what our loved one would have wanted, or couldn't provide what they needed. Again, once we cross to the Other Side we have perfect understanding and perfect peace. We have perfect forgiveness and perfect love. With extremely rare exceptions, nobody is mad over there. Over here we carry around all this baggage—we've got backpacks full of regret, doubts, and guilt. Over there, we just drop it.

God's Opinion

Lots of people, when they are feeling insecure, will try to take down somebody else to make themselves feel better. They'll seize upon something they think makes the other person different, whether it's the way they dress, the color of their skin, or even what TV show they watch or where they live. We're especially good at judging other people's mistakes. We're also really good at kicking ourselves, making judgments about ourselves, what kind of bad person we are. I'm not sure why it is that we spend so much time beating up each other and ourselves. We seem to have a very low opinion of ourselves.

Well, next to God's opinion of us, our own opinion of ourselves is not worth very much. God's opinion is the one that counts. He sees us and truly loves us unconditionally. On this side of the veil everything gets in the way of that. I think that we are here learning, experiencing, and going through all we do in the physical form to arrive at the same opinion of ourselves that God has of us. We don't have the esteem for ourselves that God does. God sees us as perfect. He sees us deserving. We beat ourselves up and He gives us unconditional love. We are here in physical form to finally get to that place where we understand and see ourselves the way God sees us, and love ourselves the way God loves us. As we get nearer to that perfection, it creates a domino effect with everything around us.

Being a spiritual person means choosing to align yourself with God, to the source of everything. Aligning yourself with God means turning on your spiritual GPS and using it. Our intuition is our connection with the Other Side, our innate knowing of what is real and true. Paying attention to our feelings, our emotions, and our intuition gives us access to the answers within ourselves.

We're really learning to become Holy God; we come here to practice. We're all here on assignment to make corrections and choices that are all based on love and to live up to God's opinion of who we really are.

People who know me will say, "Well, what about you, Concetta? You call yourself a spiritual person. How come you called that other driver a jerk? How come you called your mother-in-law a pickle-puss?"

I'm human, too. Every day, I'm trying to get better. Maybe I need one of those twelve-step programs for knee-jerk name-calling. It takes practice when you're not perfect.

Reminders and Practices

- Slow down. Focus on the here and now and give due consideration before acting or speaking. Tune in to your feelings and emotions. Listen to what they are telling you. Allow yourself to be guided to a more balanced and aware state of mind.

- Reflect on the day you've just finished. Did haste or carelessness cause you to do something you wish you hadn't? Or not do something you wish you had? Is there some way you can repair the situation?

- Sometimes we don't do what we know is the right thing because we are afraid. Fear is temporary; regret can last forever. When it's tough to do what you know is right, call on your angels for strength. Then do what is difficult.

10

Negativity

> The Mind that is too ready at contempt and reprobation
> is, I may say, as a clenched fist that can give blows, but is
> shut up from receiving and holding ought that is precious.
> —George Eliot

We all make mistakes. They usually are a thing of the moment, a snap judgment or an instant of forgetfulness. Not always, but usually, they can be rectified by bringing our conscious attention to them, by offering an apology or working to correct a wrong we've done someone. Negativity is more entrenched. A mistake is something we do once and correct; maybe we do it a couple of times before we get it and get past it. But negativity has deeper roots. It can be embedded in the personality and takes a lot more work to reverse, cleanse, and heal. It's chronic; it can be a person's whole outlook. Or it can be touched off by an event and just go on and on.

Mistakes tend to be "accidental"—we do know right from wrong and when we make a mistake we want to fix it. Anyone may be momentarily negative in difficult circumstances, but the chronically negative person suffers from a spiritual ignorance, seemingly unaware of anything larger than the moment. Their negativity seems intentional, something that's *chosen*, as difficult as this is to understand. It's not a matter of "evil," per se, but it is toxic for anyone exposed to it for any length of time.

The spiritual truth is that the negative person hurts themselves far more than they hurt anyone else. It must be like being trapped in a big black tar pit. But for those in the line of fire the effect of negativity can be anything from the annoyance of a bad wedgie—like a pair of pants or underwear you just have to keep pulling out—to something far more soul crushing. Even if you're aware that it's worse to *be* the negative person, it's not something anyone wants to be on the receiving end of.

Negativity is an inability or an unwillingness to let go of the past, an inability to forgive yourself or anyone else. An inability to connect with spirit, to trust or to love. An inability or unwillingness to consciously choose a different way, to heal a situation or oneself. It's an actual choice to keep reliving the drama. The result is such a dark heaviness that permeates the body, the home, and all one's relationships.

Dark Karma

I can't pretend to understand all the complicated ins and outs of what makes someone choose and hold on to negativity. I do know that the roots are karmic and may be an accumulation of misunderstandings, errors, or injuries from numerous lifetimes. This makes the most sense to me because what I see here is people holding on to hurts, real or imagined, seemingly without making a real effort to resolve them.

I was doing a reading at my house. The client, sitting opposite me in a high-backed chair, seemed dejected. I thought it had
been a very good reading with lots of good information, but she
didn't seem happy. Then I heard someone say, "Father." I asked
her, "Has your father crossed?" She said, "Yes, you mentioned him
already. His name is John Martin Jones." (I've changed his name
for her privacy.) In saying his whole name she did what I call "an-
nouncing" him. As she announced him, a poster in a plastic frame
that was hanging on the wall behind her literally lifted off the
wall and seemed to launch itself at her; it was only stopped from
hitting her by the high back of the chair. There's no doubt in my
mind that this was her father, actually throwing the poster. They
definitely still had an energetic connection. Their history in this
lifetime—and possibly other lifetimes, as well—was the energy
between them, and it did not look good. What she experienced
in the reading and what she seemed to be feeling in her life was, I
believe, due to her karma with her father. I sympathized with her
because I knew that she was in the middle of something that lasted
beyond death, that was going to take a lot of work to get beyond.
I always say a prayer before I begin my readings, asking God to
let only good spirits come. Once this woman left, I smudged the
whole house to clear it of any lingering dark energy.

I thought about that a lot, and I realize it sounds pretty negative for the Other Side. However, I also believe that those on that
side have the choice to be a part of the positive, to forgive and
accept forgiveness, and to receive unconditional love. I believe
that this soul is still struggling with the reality of its life spent here
and possibly can't see or has not accepted that he has done wrong.
I have heard that there are places where negative energy exists and
makes itself known. I believe these are souls that choose to still

exist with anger and distrust of God. We have a choice to become one with the love of God or not. It seems to me that God gives us this choice all the time, both here and there.

My relationship to John's family, which I've mentioned has been mostly negative for me, is certainly karmic. We are definitely part of the same Soul Group. While I don't yet know exactly what the lesson is for me, I do know there is a lesson and I'm sure that everyone involved has a part in it. Most of the time, a lesson doesn't go in just one direction. Each person is learning something.

Energy

As we talked about in chapter 4, everything is made of energy and carries energy. Energy can be positive or negative and we overlook its importance at our peril. On the Other Side they are energy experts, pure spirit, pure energy. On this side we need to learn to pay attention not only to the energy we're putting out but also the energy we're being exposed to. When it comes to negativity (negative energy) we need to be able to field the incoming as well as learn how to take control of our own.

Over the years, John's family has been so abusive to me. The last time I saw any of them was in the ShopRite. I said, "Hi, how are you?" and they literally walked by me like I was dog poop. They'll walk out of a room if I walk into it. This has been going on for years, of course, but the amazing thing is a few months ago I got an invitation in the mail for a celebratory event for one of their kids—at a church. I should have just laughed; instead I went crazy. It was like someone threw a match onto gasoline. I said, "I can't believe they'd have the audacity to send me an invitation!"

Then I tried to figure it out: "Even though I've taken years of abuse from John's family, the children have nothing to do with it.

I'd love to go celebrate a young person's accomplishments. But how could I? It's so heartbreaking. I know they don't want me there and that they'll ignore me and give me dirty looks as they've done at holidays, weddings, and any other social situation since I've been married. Maybe the deal is that they just want John there. So they'll treat John like a long-lost soldier home from war but treat me like something on the bottom of their shoe." Just thinking about it I got myself even more wound up. Initially, the energy on the envelope and the energy of the situation were affecting me. But when I gave it *more* energy, *my* energy, the energy got bigger and bigger. I started telling John's daughter, Jessica, about it: "I'll tell you right now, if your father wants to go to this he's crazy. I'm not the same girl I was thirty years ago!" Jessica said, "Don't even show it to him, just throw it out." I said, "No, I'm going to tell him. Because if he hears about it he'll wonder why I hid it from him." Anyway, long story short, when John came home I told him about it. He said to me, very calmly, "We're not going. And that's it." It really ended right there. But I was still upset over it. I was still holding on. Not only was I holding on to old, bad energy, I was putting fresh energy into it.

We do have control over our energy. If we are aware, present in the moment, we can stop this sort of thing any time we choose. But if we are not paying attention we can unwittingly contribute our own energy to the tsunami and it will just carry us along. Psychologists will tell us that if a child is neglected by a parent or both parents, very often that child will cause drama in his or her life or be disruptive to bring attention to themselves because they didn't get the attention they deserved. They're using their energy in a negative way to try to pull energy to themselves. This is a misdirection of their energy, but they're not aware of it. Awareness is the key!

We are energy, we're made up of energy, but even though we can get more energy at any given time, there isn't an unlimited amount available to us. So we need to be aware of how we're using it and not waste it on things that are negative, that do no good for us or for anyone else, or that actually even do things that are harmful and hurtful.

When something happens that is putting negative energy into contact with our own positive energy, we can intentionally block it, just refuse to participate. Like John said, "That's it." Or we can let it go wild and we can let ourselves get sick over it. When allowing negative energy to have free rein in our life becomes a pattern, getting control over it is really hard to do. When negativity becomes entrenched, what we've got to look forward to is spending the rest of our life miserable. However, if we choose, we can change the circumstances, the energy around us. Even if it means cutting ourselves off from others who are creating negative energy and want to involve us in it. You can change the effect it has on you simply by understanding that you hold the power. When negative energy invades your space you just withhold your power. You don't contribute to it. Through your focused intention, block it. And you can add an additional barricade to it by saying a prayer.

Karma

I talked earlier about the idea of banking our karma. Everything you say or do or even think is like a deposit in the Bank of Karma. If you deposit positive things—love, understanding, compassion— you can expect to be able to withdraw positive things. But our negative behaviors, words, and actions are like emptying out our account unintentionally. Like we've just handed our PIN number to some rip-off artist and we'll get no benefit from any savings we might have made.

At first, after I got that invitation, I decided to call my in-laws on the phone. I dialed the number and everything. I was actually going to say, "Are you kidding me? Why would you send me this invitation?" They didn't answer the phone. They were probably standing there looking at the caller ID. But thank God they didn't pick up, because I would have just given them even more energy. I could have contributed to that very negative energy; I could have said, "Save your stamps next time. You can kiss my butt." That's all karma. And I would have made a very bad deposit in my karma bank. Once I was able to calm my own energy down I realized I could choose not to make that kind of deposit. My deposit could be choosing to ignore it, because I already knew that if I made the other kind of deposit, that was what I was going to get back. I couldn't withdraw anything different from what I put in.

I could have taken a step even farther in the other direction. Maybe I should have called to say, "You know, we are related by marriage and we've had a really unsatisfying relationship for thirty years. I'd like to try to change that. I'd like us to be friends." To satisfy my curiosity, maybe I could have said in a calm, friendly voice, "Can you please tell me why you invited me?" I could have done that, and maybe they'd have said, "You know, Concetta, we're tired of being fools and we just wanted to be nice to you for a change." If I'd thought I would have been met with something kind or even just honest, it would have been worth the phone call. But I knew that was not going to happen. There are some who will keep making the negative deposits because they don't know how to say, "I'm sorry." If someone says to me, "Concetta, I'm sorry I hurt you," I'm going to say, "That's all right. And if I hurt you, I'm sorry, too." It's easy for me to extend an apology or to reciprocate when one has been extended to me. But there are some who are just incapable of admitting any fault or wrongdoing. And being a nice person, trying to make the right sort of deposits in the Bank of Karma, does not require that we hang out with people who take an ugly pleasure in making us feel bad. We can just reject this kind of energy and look for other prospects. We just say, "No, it's not our policy to accept this kind of contribution. You'll have to take that elsewhere."

Karmically, I know I can't change these people, but I can do my utmost to at least keep peace in my own home.

Over the last twenty-eight years, I've continually second-guessed myself. I don't want to be unfair, but I've never seen any evidence that they've regarded me in any way other than as the person who poisoned John's mind and destroyed their family. Since we really have not had any resolution of whatever the issues were, I continue to carry this weight with me. I think about it all the time and try to remain open to any inspiration about what might be done to repair things. But it's very hard to do from just one side—it's true it takes two to tango and both parties need to participate. Absent that, we can only pray for our own peace of mind and make our best effort to treat others the way we'd want to be treated. I have found peace. I made a choice to be happy, and I *am* happy with John and with the people I share my life with. I am happy to have a loving relationship with Jessica, whom I love as my very own daughter and who I know loves me—even to the point of protecting me from myself (after all, she's the one who said to throw away the letter as if I'd never even received it!). I know for sure that there are reasons for this situation, lessons from all of this for each of us. I know for sure there is something beyond this that requires we ultimately get understanding and get to the point of love.

Allies on the Other Side

All of us have angels looking after us. Especially when we are doing our best to combat negativity in our lives.

One day when John and I had been married only a short time and were really having problems—most of them stirred up by my in-laws—I was in the shower and I heard from someone I had never met. John's father, Leo, had died when John was in his early twenties. John and his father had never had a man-to-man relationship. His dad had been an alcoholic and had used John to cover for him on occasion when he was drinking. Definitely not a case of the parent taking care of the child. But, having crossed to the Other Side, Leo now had understanding of his errors and wanted to help his son. To do that, he reached out to me. His manner was very kind and he reassured me that things would get better. He urged me to just hang in there. The family dysfunction had been so entrenched that in those difficult days, I really doubted John would ever be able to break away from it. But in fact his father was right. John did open his eyes to the truth and he did change, and things did get better. I believe that Leo was probably working both ends in this, maybe showing things to John in his dreams as well as communicating with me.

John's father has been a constant help to me. When John and I were arguing a lot during the early years of our marriage, Leo would come by and tell me kind things to help keep me in balance with the situation. He loved his son and is dealing with his regrets on the Other Side by helping John here. We'll probably never know all of the help he gives us.

Along with Leo, I had other support and good advice. Mushy was one of my greatest sources of comfort, always willing to listen. One Saturday she was at my house teaching me to make curtains out of sheets. She is so talented with so many things that I'm not. John came in the house and the tension between us was so great, anyone could feel it. Mushy told me that it brought her back to her second marriage, a very unhappy one; she told me she saw the same thing happening between John and me. She felt that there was hope for us, that John was different, and maybe I just couldn't see it. She showed me that I was involved in the negative energy and told me that divorce was a certainty in the near future if I didn't change my view. Her counsel made me stop and think, and realize what I had sunk to and become. It took a few days for me to analyze her words . . . but soon I knew she was right. I *trusted* her. I had become so full of anger that I was treating John poorly. He was living in a cloud and couldn't see the result of years of conditioning from his family, but my treating him poorly did not help anything. Mushy made me realize I had to change my ways, get back to who I was when I first met John, and let him know who I am, not what they had caused me to become. At the very moment of this realization things started to change. It did take time, but John and I were able to get back to the spirit of who we had been to each other and grow even closer from that point on.

I realize not everyone has the ability to hear their father-in-law in the shower, but if you find yourself caught up in your own ongoing negative circumstances I urge you to pay attention to your dreams and keep your eyes open for the teachers all around you in your life. A teacher could be a good friend whose opinion you value, or it could be a scene enacted in front of you among strangers in a subway car or at some public event. Maybe what you are seeing is a positive example of something you could try with your own situation. Or it might be an example of negative behavior reminding you this is not how you want to behave. When such a scene catches your attention it's not happenstance—remember all the directors and producers are on the Other Side. It's another way the Other Side can send you a message to convey something you need to know, help you make a decision, or simply provide moral support.

If You're Trapped in Negativity

Negativity can be triggered by a loss, an accident, or an illness that places us in a position of sadness or difficulty that we feel helpless against. Or it can spring from something as small as a disappointment—something we wanted that we didn't get. Everyone suffers many disappointments in a human lifetime, but in some cases the individual is unable to pull themselves out of the darkness—they are either unwilling or just can't. When we make a mistake it's certainly possible to make it worse, but while it may affect another person, it usually won't take on a life of its own, in a sense *infecting* others around us. Not so with negativity. When negativity rears its head, others can easily be taken down.

A friend I'll call Ann was going through a divorce—something often so incredibly stressful that it brings out the worst in everyone. Ann and her husband have three children—two boys and one girl, all now of legal age. Although I'm better friends with Ann I've known them as a couple over the years and to be honest, they never seemed particularly loving to one another; they always seemed to me to have some distance between them. So when she left him I wasn't that surprised. She told me she stayed in the relationship all those years for her children. Both Ann and her estranged husband have legal backgrounds, so you can imagine that since she told him she wanted a divorce it had been "game on."

The first complication was that Ann came in line to inherit a large amount of money from her mother. Her husband went nuts—not out of love for her, but out of love for the money she stood to inherit. He set out to hurt her badly (his negative antics are too long to list!), and through his own negativity he turned her sons and daughter against her. He played the victim and told them horrible things about their mother. Ann has been so hurt by the things that have been said and done to her by her children. Even little things. For example, Ann has been so supportive of one of her sons who played football. She attended every game and brought food for her son and the other players and knew everyone involved with his team. She looked forward to the day when she'd get to take part in a ceremony where the parents of the players walk onto the field with their kids and the mothers receive flowers from their sons. But on that day, the boy told her not to come on the field. He said, "Dad is coming." Her husband received the flowers from their son, as Ann sat on the sideline crying. I helped walk her through this, letting her know what the Other Side was saying, that this would take time but things would get better, that people would come to see the truth.

And of course that has happened. The boys, at least, have found out more of the facts of the whole situation and have come around. Unfortunately, their daughter is still under her father's negative spell. I believe that in the core of the daughter's soul she knows the truth about the way she is treating her mother. She's been manipulated by her father, who should have known better. He wanted to hurt Ann and he used his own children, not realizing he was hurting them—even to the point where he's helped his daughter to mess up her own karma. He'll have to live with this—it'll be a correction for him down the road. These are smart, educated people. Sometimes I say, "Stupid is stupid; ya can't fix stupid." But with folks we consider intelligent, we have to ask ourselves, what is wrong with this picture?

Say, "I'm Sorry"

As with mistakes, there is a simple tool available to us and that is just apologizing and asking for forgiveness. "I'm sorry" is such a powerful first step in counteracting negativity as long as it is offered sincerely and doesn't simply become a glib fallback for a repeat offender.

I believe Ann's daughter got in so deep that now she does not know how to go back. Amazing, isn't it? Just a simple "I am sorry I hurt you" would open the door. "I love you. I miss you." But she cannot figure out how to get out of this mess. Again, like Dorothy in Oz, she has to find the answers herself. All of us have to face and make choices. We need to school ourselves to see the big picture, step outside of our own pain and anger. It's not easy for anyone; often it's something that must be worked on our entire lives. The Other Side is always walking us through our good and bad times here, providing us with opportunities to make better choices.

Even knowing what I know it's really no easier to keep from hearing negative things in my head. I don't want to be a jack-off (that was Howard Stern's way of putting it to keep from getting fined by the FCC); I want to be a good person. But I'm human. Even someone we might look up to, like Betty Ford or Barack Obama—they've had the same human struggle. I don't have more than my share of perfect days and I know that every day is not perfect for others—not on this side of the veil. You are not the only person who's having the rug pulled out from under them.

I don't see any apology forthcoming from Ann's husband. Even if he could recognize the damage he's done and feel remorse, I believe ego is playing a role here. (EGO = Edging God Out.) I'd like to be proven wrong. We're all susceptible to our own negativity and the influence of others. But we always have the opportunity to say sorry and try again to do right. It's surprising how many people feel incapable of doing this but it's really necessary.

Reaping What We Sow

I realize we are not always conscious of the damage we're doing. Especially if we grew up in dysfunctional surroundings, negativity can be so ingrained we perpetuate it unconsciously. But even if we aren't aware, we are adversely affecting our karma when we are the cause of this kind of bad energy. One way or another, we reap what we sow.

We need to pay attention not only to the good things we do intentionally, but to the bad things we do unintentionally. Sometimes you say to yourself, "I'm only going to plant tomatoes this year," and then there's corn that comes up out of your compost pile all by itself. The whole garden is our responsibility. What's getting thrown on the compost pile that might take it upon itself to come up, even if you don't want it to? Are there weeds in there that will start to choke the vegetables you've planted?

I don't know what is going to happen next. Ann's daughter has some conscious choices to make and some weeding to do. I believe it might take many years. Her daughter is only twenty-four now. She may have to really grow up, get married herself, have children, and go through some pain of her own—find out what comes up in her garden that she wasn't expecting—to understand what she did wrong. There's a lot of karma involved in this situation that took only one year to test *all* of them.

Sit quietly, calmly, and visualize all your negative thoughts about a person or a situation as a dark, black cloud. Maybe the cloud has little smoky trails to it and you need to mentally gather all of these together. See these strands coming together, the cloud getting denser and denser, the cloud growing smaller, as all the negativity is gathered into it and compressed. Then picture this tiny dark cloud floating out of the left side of your brain. It's important to clearly visualize it because this puts energy in motion. Be careful that no one is sitting near you on your left side as you do this, as you don't want to bathe them in your negativity!

Next, consider what you would like your relationship to the person or situation to be. Design and visualize your ideal situation (imagine bright, cheerful colors) and place this image on a fluffy white cloud to your right and allow those new thoughts, this new reality, to float in via the right side of your brain. Enjoy this image for a while. Breathe deeply and smile.

Ask for Protection

I was visiting a dear friend at her beach house, and in the course of our conversation, she shared with me that she had been abused for many years when she was a girl by her own brother. Her parents, if they knew, pretended not to notice, and in her household it was just taken as a given that the son walked on water and could do no wrong. Many years later, her brother accidentally outed himself at a family dinner. There was an argument and for once he was taking some heat. In the course of it he blurted out, "I know she's told you that I abused her, but it isn't true!" Well, she, of course, had never said a word, so now everyone was looking at him like, where'd that come from? And suddenly he'd created a suspicion where before nobody had a clue. Still, her parents didn't do anything. It wasn't until a long time later that finally her mother asked her one day, "Is it true?" and she said, "Yes, it's true." But still nobody said anything to her brother; nobody did anything. As far as the parents were concerned the brother was still a god, and she just lives with that fact. My friend herself is a very psychologically healthy person, a very spiritual and healing person, who works to help others heal and find peace, but she carries this with her. I have to say I was very upset learning that she had been treated so badly and her parents, whom she never said a bad word about, were, in the end, complicit—that's how it seemed to me. I really was furious on her behalf. I said, "Honey, forgive me, I know they're your parents, but how can you just live with this and not feel any anger toward them?" I realize that I'm passing judgment on them and they're both dead. My friend loves her parents very much— she was visibly upset that they had not done anything to rescue her when she needed them, but she was really trying to find peace with them about this matter.

At this point, my friend got up from where we'd been sitting to get something and a bottle of wine that had been standing up-right toward the back of the kitchen counter suddenly slid forward off the counter, hit the corner of the woodstove, and smashed. It seemed the parents, now on the Other Side, did not appreciate her telling me this story, or they may not have appreciated the lack of sympathy I had toward them. What I sensed intuitively was that they knew they were wrong not to have protected my friend from her brother, but they didn't want me to judge them—they were actually defending themselves.

Normally once a spirit gets to the Other Side, if they've done something wrong to someone who is still over here they will try to make amends, they'll try to do a good turn for that person. But not always; sometimes the spirit has not learned as much as they need to, and sometimes it can take a while for them to understand the damage they've done, so there may still be a period after they cross when the spirit is literally healing themselves from negativity they've carried on this side. When I'm doing a reading or when I'm just in contact with a spirit because I am with someone that spirit knows, I don't know the whole history between the spirit and the individual here. The person here will know, but the spirit there is communicating, too—in their own way, they are shouting to get their message through.

While I've certainly experienced it, this degree of lingering negativity is not at all common. You don't have some version of the Amityville Horror stirring up on the Other Side and shooting back to this side. I always make every effort to keep clear of these unevolved, negative spirits. And anyone who is experiencing this kind of turbulence, such as objects moving around them in a threatening way, can use some protection. Simply say aloud or in prayer, "In the name of God, take that dark energy away from me, remove that dark energy from my home." Or say, "Michael the archangel, take up your mighty sword and protect me from this dark energy." Or send out your message to "all the angels" or to whomever or whatever makes you feel safe. It doesn't matter what your religion is, or if you have no religion in particular. It's still the same all-knowing, all-loving force that responds and intervenes on your behalf.

I've been asked whether negative energy can ever be so strong that you literally have to leave your home. I'd have to say it's possible; energy can linger, the bad like the good. One time we were visited by someone who I knew very well did not like me and when this individual left, not all their energy left with them. But you can always rid yourself of this by saying prayers or asking God for protection, and you also can smudge your home with sage or incense while you ask for protection and help in getting rid of the negativity.

Put the Positive in Motion

A lot of times our low-level negative behaviors stem from not feeling good about ourselves. I don't know why this is, but it seems to be the case that when we're feeling bad we want to bring everyone down with us. For many people, if they're not happy about themselves—if they don't *love* themselves—then, even if it's unconsciously, they don't want others to be happy or to love themselves. We need to be proactive—not just about warding off incoming negativity, but also about putting out *positive* energy!

Our words and actions are all energy and so are our thoughts. Someone who is holding on to negative thoughts about themselves will automatically create that for themselves and around themselves. I'm not happy to say that in the work I do I meet so many people who have very low self-confidence. One of my favorite things to tell people is that you've gotta look in the mirror at some point in the day—to comb your hair, wash your face, shave, brush your teeth, whatever you have to do—so while you're there, look into your own eyes and visualize your own beauty. *Put your energy in motion* by saying, "I am beautiful." Do it regularly. Repeat it, repeat it, repeat it until you get it. Until you *are* it. Using your own energy, you design your own creation, yourself, your circumstances. We can get up and look around us and say, "Oh shoot. Look at what didn't go right. Look, it's raining. I have nothing to wear. My hair looks like crap. Oh, I have to talk to so-and-so today and I know he's not going to be happy with what I have to tell him." You are creating that. Instead, try saying something positive: "Look at how beautiful and green everything is from the rain. I love my hair and it looks fabulous."

We get up every day and put ourselves, our energy, in motion. We climb out of bed and we're already in motion. Whatever we do with our energy through our physical body, that's what we are making happen. Our thoughts are the same way. It's still our energy with which we are creating everything. What is so hard to understand is that as we are thinking we are bringing our energy-in-motion to situations and circumstances, just like we are when we move our body and make things happen. So many people walk through their days, their lives, thinking they aren't in control of it (and because they're thinking this, they're not!). If we get an invitation in the mail that upsets us, that pisses us off, there's a way to get around it. Say, "I'm not going to give it the energy that I once did." This is how I handle it: Throw it away; it's done. Don't obsess over it. Believe me, I am obsessive; I know that. And I work very hard to control it. If I can control it, I'm pretty sure anyone can.

Blessings at the Core

We all need to deal with ordinary negativity. Every life has rain. We all have challenges—that's what the earth plane is all about. Negativity is a reality of the physical plane. The idea is to not let it linger and, if possible, not pass it on to anyone else. At the core of our soul is an abundance of blessings. But on top of that we have all this different crap that gets in the way—our negative thoughts, our issues and judgments. As we work on our lessons, we begin to get rid of the crap, uncovering the blessings. But when the blessings start bubbling to the top, sometimes we get frightened and stuff them back down. It feels too good; some of us aren't used to that, so we start to worry about feeling too good and we stuff the positive feelings down and let the crap cover it over again. We dwell on the crap. We create negative dramas that keep us stuck in our spiritual development, and frankly keep us from experiencing all the happiness we could have here on earth.

All of us have abandonment issues. We've all been victims, neglected; we've all thought at one time or another that we'd nearly die because of things that have happened to us in our life. We all bring the past into the present. We need to learn how to have these experiences, get the lessons, and then let go of the bad feelings. If we feel we've been wronged, trying to hurt another person or get back at them is only going to mess up our own karma. We need to avoid the temptation we might feel to stoke the drama, wallow in the tar pit of negativity. I say, embrace all the events in your life—call yourself a survivor and claim the victory. Any event is temporary. We can experience the event, remember the event, but cut off the emotion and still claim the victory. Don't hold on to some bad thing that happened like it's a claims ticket to justice.

Reminders and Practices

- What bad event do you recall, do you dwell on, that is only causing you pain? Can you think of a way to release it, to let it go?

- Close your eyes and picture yourself as the calm at the center of the storm. No matter how crazy things are all around you, you do not contribute your energy to that. Instead, visualize healing energy moving outward from all sides of the center where you are, vaporizing negativity as it goes.

- If you are feeling under attack from another person's negative energy, practice intentionally blocking this. Say, "Stop right there," and offer your angels a prayer to guard you.

11

Enough

Lives based on having are less free than lives based on doing or on being.

—William James

———

Everyone is trying to accomplish big things not realizing life is made up of little things.

—Frank "Parson" Clark

A woman came to see me whose parents both had crossed. Her father had died and she was so upset about his passing, and then her mother died soon after. When I was doing the reading her mother came through and asked me to tell her, "Good luck with the car." She hadn't driven that day—someone else brought her to my home for the reading—but she was blown away by the message because she said the one thing her mother had kept saying to her when she was alive was to get herself a Mercedes. You know, get herself a very special car. She'd say, "Just go buy yourself one!" Her mother always wanted her to do it, and she could afford it, but she never would. After her mother died, she finally went and got the car. When she was picking up the car at the dealership, she told me, she noticed that the date on the car was her mother's birthday. No coincidence, of course, and something she couldn't help smiling about.

This is the physical plane, the material world we are living in—the plane of stuff. Part of what we learn here by manipulating and playing with physical objects is what is necessary and what is not. In the physical body we have physical needs for food, shelter, and clothes—the basics. Over millennia we've developed tools to help us get, grow, or make those things. From the earliest days of humans we've decorated our bodies, hair, and clothing for ceremonial purposes, to show status, to express our unique sense of style, or simply for fun. Pretty much everything in human development has run from the simplest form to a high level of complexity, and we look at places in the world that don't have this complexity, or even sometimes all the basics, and call them "undeveloped" or the "third world." Here, someone might be thinking they'd like to redo their bathroom to have a jumbo walk-in shower with side jets and six settings on the showerhead; there they may not even have clean water to drink. I see so many people, not only in my practice but just around me in life generally, who seem always to be striving for something more than what they already have. As we develop spiritually, we need to come to an understanding of what is really important, what is really enough.

Looking for Peace

The first point I want to make is that it is not a crime to want and get stuff. You don't have to drive some junker if you want and can afford a Mercedes. It's okay to want more money than you have—to have a nicer home or a great vacation or pay for college or a wedding or whatever. It's individual to each person, but to cut right to the chase, what all of us really are after is peace. Everything else is stuff in the middle—peace is the end goal. No matter what extra we want in our life, whether it's a new refrigerator or a new relationship, it's because we believe it will bring us a sense of fulfillment, contentment, ease, satisfaction, completion—peace.

The big question is, what is it that will bring us to peace? While there really is only one answer to this question ultimately, we have to understand that this side of the veil operates through illusion, so it *seems* that the answer is different for each person, depending on where they are in their spiritual journey. If we have what feels like a hole in our soul—we feel we are lacking something—we will try to fill it with pretty much anything at hand or anything suggested to us. This is what marketing experts know—all they need to do is suggest to us that what they are selling will bring us peace (whether in the form of self-esteem or the promise of love) and we'll knock ourselves out trying to figure out how to get it. In reality, the hole is a God-shaped hole and the only thing that will fill it and bring us peace is God. But before we truly recognize and understand that—and it can take us innumerable lifetimes to really get it—we try to fill that emptiness with everything else. We're learning here; it's a process. So much of this is purely experimentation. It's not just allowed but expected that while we are here we will have "desires," if you will, that there will be things we want and will try to get—then we can see through our own experience whether or not they were really worth having.

So Let the Games Begin

Pretty much anything we really want here we can get, and the Other Side is only too happy to help. But whatever you're after, it's not going to come gift-wrapped to your doorstep without your making an effort. The process isn't difficult to grasp, but because we're easily distracted, it can be tough to master.

Rule #1

Begin with a positive mind-set.

It's silly to even have to say this, but you need to start out certain that your efforts will be effective. Thought is energy and will affect your outcome. If you're thinking that you won't have a positive outcome, you're right—because your very thoughts will prevent the positive outcome.

Rule #2

Don't give the universe mixed signals!

Doesn't everybody know someone like this? The woman who says, "Oh, I don't care if I never get married. I don't really want to meet a man. I don't need the aggravation; I like having time to myself." Then in another moment, she says, "Well, I really am lonely, I'd really like to meet somebody nice." Be clear in your intention. You need to keep repeating the exact thing you want. You can't give mixed signals to the universe.

Again, it's energy, the energy contained in your thoughts, that you are putting out there, and if you're being inconsistent, the energy is confused—it's not one thing or another, it's both. If you keep changing your mind, maybe you'll meet someone, but it won't work out because you're still on the fence and your energy is still on the fence.

Rule #3
Reinforce your intention.

Don't worry about repeating too often what you are looking for. The Other Side is not going to get bored of hearing you. They just want you to trust them, have confidence and patience. You don't have to repeat what you're after two hundred times a day; you just have to repeat it whenever you think of it. If it comes to your mind, give the same consistent thought. Again, you can't switch back and forth on what you really desire. It would be like my saying to the universe as I'm working on a book, "Gee, I'd love to have another *New York Times* bestseller," but then the next day thinking, "Well, it doesn't really matter. I already have one." And then the next day, "No, no, no—I want another one." Any time my mind drifts off to my next book, all finished and in the stores, I'm going to say, "Yes, I want a *New York Times* bestseller. That's really what I want. I want so many people to read this and learn all of this and make their lives better and the world better. Yup. Make 'er a *New York Times* bestseller." It has to be consistent.

Rule #4
Put it in action.

You have to be positive and you have to repeat it. And you have to put it all into action. I'm not going to have a bestselling book unless I first write the book. If you are saying, "I'd like to meet someone," you can't lock yourself in your house every night with the TV on. On the physical plane we need to employ physical means. Yes, we are energy, but we are energy being directed through a physical medium, the human body. And I think you'd agree with me that when you say you'd like to meet a guy, you're talking about a physical guy, not a ghost, right? So you need to put your own physical body where you can encounter the guy's physical body. You have to say, "I'd like to meet somebody. Maybe I'll go to that party and maybe I'll meet somebody there." Give them the chance! The Other Side and all your helpers over there are going to try to help you out. But you need to give them the opportunity to create a meeting for you. The only guy they can bring you if you're sitting on your couch watching TV is the guy delivering the pizza or the sushi or whatever you ordered. Or maybe the cable guy. If that's the guy you're looking for, then sure, you're giving the universe clear signals and you're giving the Other Side the chance it needs to bring you the guy of your dreams—"I want a guy but I don't want to leave the couch to find him." "Okay, here he is!" But if you aren't looking for the delivery guy or the cable guy then you need to get yourself to a place where you feel safe and friendly.

Rule #5
Give it a boost.

We can use tools to enhance the energy behind our intentions—prayer, saying a mantra, meditation, visualization, journaling. All of these are different ways of focusing, amplifying, and broadcasting our clear intention and desire.

To focus their prayer, someone might use rosary beads, someone else might burn incense to focus their mantra, and another person might hold in their hand a special stone or feather. We hold on to these objects as reminders, to bring us to a pure place in our heart. Finding a special spot that you feel energetically in tune with—whether it's a church or somewhere in nature—can also help you focus and fine-tune your energy and send the universe a clear message of what it is you truly want.

Bear in mind, however, that places we might consider special or sacred are not the only places where we can invoke help or ask the Other Side for assistance to bring us something we badly want or need. You could be at a bus stop, on a train, waiting in a doctor's office. The only thing of real importance is that you quiet your mind. If you're thinking eight hundred thoughts at one time you'll confuse the energy. You need to send a focused thought. It doesn't matter if you are in a holy place or holding on to a holy object. So long as you are quiet in your mind, wherever you are, you are talking to the Holy Spirit, directly to God. You can do it anywhere. I'm not a regular churchgoer so this is how I most often will send out my own wishes and dreams.

You can also create a vision board—cut pictures from a magazine or get a photograph that reminds you of the thing you really want and look at it and dream about it. Picture yourself already having it, whatever it is. Picture yourself walking on a beautiful beach in Hawaii, if that's what you want, with the guy or gal of your dreams. You can also write down your desires in a journal, or take a little piece of paper and roll it up and put it in a small container. I'm not going to suggest you put a message in a bottle and drop the bottle in the ocean, because that's just littering and we've got enough of that—don't get me started! But you can put it in some other little container—a jewelry box, a potpourri or ginger jar. A friend of mine has a beautiful gourd from Peru with designs carved into the sides and a lid carved into the top. She writes down what she wants and folds it up and puts the message in this gourd and never takes it out—and she's told me that more often than not the thing she's wished for has arrived in due time.

Flow and Abundance

If you follow these simple rules, the Other Side will deliver. You can't take it with you, but you can certainly enjoy it while you are here. So many people still seem to cling to that whole "He who dies with the most toys wins" philosophy and look to find their happiness in getting everything they have coming to them and more. But everything here comes and goes. I've never seen a Brink's truck in a funeral procession.

When a loved one dies there can be real unhappiness, with conflicts over "who gets what"—I see it all the time in my practice. What I also see, however, is how unimportant "stuff" is to the Other Side and to our spiritual well-being here. I have many stories of souls who have either expressed their concerns over their living loved ones' greed or have told me of their sincere gratitude that their family members have realized how little "things" are worth compared to their relationships, preserving harmony, or giving someone else pleasure.

One story I especially love is that of a woman who had lost her mother. During the reading the mother came through and showed me lots of hats and costume jewelry—I mean a *lot!* Boxes and boxes of these things. The mother went on to show me a little girl who passed from cancer. She gave the name of the little girl; however, I didn't see her as a relative. After a long reading my client told me that her mother had had tons of fake jewelry and lots of hats. When her mother passed, she, the daughter, had donated all of this to a children's hospital for the sick children to play with. I'm certain the child the mother introduced during the reading was one of those children, who had since died and came through to thank this woman for giving them those lovely things to play with.

As I've already said, it's way okay to ask for things here; it's fine to have a life full of beautiful stuff. Material things are for the living; the dead have zero use for them. But it's also important to keep things moving along. Anything we have here comes from God the Creator and as we are really ultimately spirit and need nothing material, nothing here on earth ever permanently belongs to us. Things come into our care for a short time. We enjoy them then pass them on for others to enjoy. The spiritual idea is not to become attached to the stuff, but to let it pass through us. We're not an empty bucket to fill; we're more like a channel through which all things we want or need may flow abundantly.

Some people, no matter how much they have, always feel they are lacking. They are simply unable to feel a sense of having enough, let alone the relaxed and expansive feeling of having abundance. The source of their dissatisfaction (or even pain), however, does not come from what they have or don't have. It isn't anything external at all. The cause of this pain is a hole in their very soul. It may be because they were never valued in their family that they never developed a sense of being okay just as who and what they are. To varying degrees we all suffer from this—it's a hand-me-down curse. We learned it from our parents, from society, from the media. We compare ourselves to everyone else and find it hard to acknowledge that we have what we need and are happy when we're constantly shown images of what we are supposed to want. A hole in the soul cannot be filled with money or stuff. If we don't already respect ourselves it can't even be filled with the respect of others. It can only be filled by remembering that we are a part of God, that His love fills us and surrounds us. This releases our true identity and self-esteem. Again, it can be a lifetime's process, or many lifetimes' process, to learn or remember this. The irony is that where we fail to feel abundant from *getting* more, we can feel abundant by *giving* more. We don't have to get more on the outside, we need to get more on the inside and give more on the outside.

There's an old story about a man who visits a small village. Of the first person he comes to he asks, "Would you show me your most spiritual citizen?" The person takes him to see a smiling old fellow living in a tiny, nearly empty home. He then asks to be shown the village's richest citizen. On the way into the village he'd spotted a huge house on a hill and asked his impromptu guide if that was where the richest person lived. "No, no," his guide told him. "That's where the old miser lives. You've already met our richest citizen—the one who has given everything away."

I think the point of the story is clear—what makes us rich is not having the most but being the most like God, giving of ourselves and what we have to others. When we are able to share, this is true abundance.

> You can avoid excess and waste if you take the time to consider what you ask for and what you choose to keep. Ask yourself, "Is this beautiful—does it uplift my spirits? Do have I a need for it? Does it hold important memories for me? Does it bring me enjoyment? Or can it teach me something?"

Caring and Karma

Our karma and our intended life lessons play a role in virtually every aspect of our lives. A particular lesson we are here to work on can affect what we have in this lifetime, although our free will while we are here can overrule this. If what we decide we want once we are here is different from what we originally agreed to, it can be a little difficult to make the change because in essence we'll be somewhat at war with ourselves over it, at least subconsciously. But, again, free will has the last say so long as we then remain consistent. Our karma also can affect our situation and prospects greatly—what we are "born into" and what we may attain. But there's another element of our karma that will have a distinct affect that is only partly to do with our past lives and everything we do here and now: Do we show ourselves as *deserving* of what we have? Do we, by our actions, *earn* more?

I'm not talking about earning things by the sweat of our brow (although it may be necessary to do some work!). What I'm talking about is, do we show ourselves to have a generous spirit? Do we know how to share? Do we take care of what is put into our hands? Are these things we've already learned? If we've shown ourselves in the past to be destructive or have a grasping nature, there are some corrections due in this area. But if we show that we've learned to share with others, that we know how to care for people and things or we've worked to restore something that has been damaged (be it a relationship, a bicycle, a broken teapot, a child's skinned knee, or a city park), we're demonstrating a worthiness to have things of value.

Respect and Appreciation

I can't stand to see litter and trash everywhere in our world. It's not just in our cities. In fact, some city streets are remarkably clean considering how many people are living so close together. But I see trash everywhere—yes, along the street and sidewalks and parking lots, but also in the park, at the beach, even in the woods.

When I was a child there was not so much trash. I grew up in a rural area of New Jersey, so I remember a cleaner world, green and beautiful. Most of us, when I was a girl, didn't have so much stuff. Now everything is instant and disposable. Even if the "stuff" itself isn't disposable, it probably came wrapped in something that is. I really feel that the more we get sometimes, the less respect we have for it. Like something that comes too easily to us. Why should that be?

Think about how you feel if you give someone a gift and they don't seem to care about it. Maybe you bought a new shirt for your husband and he just leaves it hanging in his closet with the tags on it, it falls on the floor when he's pulling something else out to wear, and he doesn't even notice that he steps on it as he's backing away from the closet. Are you going to buy him another shirt any time soon? Maybe some seventeen-year-old is given a new car as a graduation gift and goes out first thing and carelessly gets into a wreck. They aren't being careful because they have no notion of the work that paid for that car—they weren't out there mowing lawns or flipping burgers to make the payments. Now the parents may say, "You have to pay to get it fixed," or "You have to get a job if you want a new car." Either way, they didn't respect the gift enough to give it due care, so it entails a correction; now if they want a nice car they have to roll up their own sleeves. This can go for any kind of gift. What if you gave money to a charity that you believed in and you saw that your money is just going to pay the salaries of a few people at the top instead of to the charity's stated purpose, or used to print and mail more solicitations to ask you for more money, or just simply wasted? You'd probably think, "I'm never giving them money again. They don't use it for the work they say they're doing so my handing them my hard-earned cash is not making an improvement. Let them have a bake sale next time!"

Nobody likes to see their gift disrespected, wasted, or ruined.

We're all created in God's image, so don't you think God might feel similarly? "I gave you a beautiful planet and you trashed it. You're just going to have to clean it up yourself." There are many, many individual souls who have serious karmic corrections to make in this area; in fact, there are many, many entire Soul Link Groups around the globe that need to get to work on this. We all need to do our part to restore the beauty of God's gift to us.

We have to learn to respect both what we work for and what we are just blessed with. And maybe the way to appreciate what we have is to have to work for everything, even for our blessings. We trash the world we were blessed with, we're going to have to work to clean it up. But the secret is that whenever we do this, we're not just making our world more beautiful, we are making ourselves more beautiful, and as we show ourselves as more beautiful in spirit, more deserving, we open ourselves up to even greater blessings. There's a mutuality involved when we give ourselves over to the work of *caring* for what God has given us. It shows that we *appreciate* all our great gifts, that we respect God and what He has given us. It shows God that we are making our best effort to align ourselves with His will. What I mean is, in a real sense, we are *giving* to Him by *caring* for what He has given us and we show ourselves as worthy to receive His blessings. Am I saying that God only blesses the deserving or worthy? No, certainly not. Anyone with eyes in their head can see that God blesses us all.

Keep It Simple, Sweetheart

Here on this side of the veil there's so much focus put on "supersizing" everything. No house is big enough, no deal is big enough, no meal is big enough, no party is off the hook enough. We live in such fast times with such enormous expectations. There's so much pressure to do more, be more, have more—we create so much stress for ourselves. This much pressure can lead to addictions, and we can be addicted to pretty much anything—food, drugs, alcohol, tanning, exercise, praise, attention. How much do we really need and what is really important? Who are we trying to impress? From everything I've ever heard from the Other Side, as well as from everything I've learned on this side, I'd like to let you in on a secret: Not everything has to be a big freaking deal.

If we put our minds to it, can't we think of a million small delights and comforts? A giggle with a friend; a hot shower after shoveling snow; receiving a real letter in the mail; seeing a movie that actually moves us; sweet, clean drinking water; holding a newborn baby, kitten, or puppy; that wonderful feeling in your mouth after you have brushed your teeth; the smell of roses from your garden; the feel of the sand under your feet at the beach; having a dream of a loved one who has passed looking very peaceful; watching birds eating seeds at the feeder; the sound of children laughing . . . or how about enjoying a good bowl of pasta!

A great deal of our unhappiness is created because we cannot look around us and understand how perfectly amazing and special our lives are, how amazing and special the world is—these amazing and special gifts from God. Think about what impresses a child—playing outside in the summer sunshine, lying in the grass, petting or holding a baby animal, finding an unusual leaf or bug, having their dad or mom play with them and give them their full attention.

In my readings for clients, most often it is little things that the dead will want to remind them of—the small connections, the jokes they shared, a simple experience they had together. If we're ever going to be happy here we need to find appreciation for and satisfaction in the simple things in life; we need to learn how to be open to more enjoyment in smaller "bites."

The other night I was doing a reading for a client and I said to her, "Why is it I keep seeing lightning then rain, then lightning, then rain?" I almost didn't want to say it, because I was thinking, "What the heck is this?" But then the young woman I was reading for told me about a grandmother she was very close to who'd passed away. Her grandmother loved watching the weather, and she especially loved a big rainstorm. She used to sit on the outside back porch of her house—she lived by the river—and she'd say, "Come on, honey. Let's go watch it," and they'd watch the lightning and the rain bounce off the river. I said, "Wow, that's so sweet."

It's so difficult on this side of the veil; we really need to learn to relax. Do I feel that there is nothing in the world worth stressing over? Not at all. But I also know the value of not buying in to the pressure of the modern world to always think things have to be bigger and better by somebody else's standard. I'd argue there's real value in taking a job that pays $18,000 a year if you can pay your bills with that and it's something that makes you truly happy.

Gratitude for What Is Ours

I never had children of my own. This was something the Other Side told me about when I was really young, that I would not get to experience being a mother. Even having been told this, though, I still fought against it. I tried everything I could do to change that verdict, but to give birth to my own child was just not my path in this lifetime. I was so angry for many years—all through my thirties I was terribly angry. But the Holy Spirit blessed me anyway. He brought me a wonderful man to marry who had two children from his previous marriage, and I loved these kids so much that I came to think of them as and call them my own. I know the difference. They have their own mother—my husband's ex-wife. I'm not confused about that. But for all intents and purposes, I still feel that they were brought to me to love as my own. My husband's daughter, Jessica, *my* daughter, is my best friend. I'm so grateful to God for bringing her and my son, John (my husband John's son), into my life.

We're never going to be happy if we judge ourselves by what we haven't got, if we feel jealousy over someone else's lot in life— their possessions, relationships, or abilities. We are all in this game together and sometimes we need to wait our turn. Sometimes there's simply another plan that we ourselves, along with God, set in motion that we've forgotten about but is in our best interests. When it comes to what others have, better exercises would be to practice appreciation for what draws you to those things, per- haps emulate the best qualities of the people who have them, and be generous with your compliments. No one loves a green-eyed monster and we only make ourselves sick when we begrudge and covet. We can ask the universe to help us fill any void we feel, but the surest way to receive is to give. This includes, most especially, giving thanks.

Nothing is "insufficient." We are enough, we have enough. If a cup of water is taken from a stream, the rest of the stream adjusts to the loss of that cup of water. Pour it back in, and again the stream adjusts to make room for its return. With or without that cup of water, the stream is complete; it is enough.

Regardless of what you have or have not at the moment, both spiritually and materially, you can have it all. God's gift to us is unlimited abundance—we all can think of things we want, but at the heart of it we all want peace. That's what we think we'll have when we have enough money, when we have the love of our dreams or the home of our dreams. It's really what everyone is looking for here on earth that we won't have perfectly until we reach heaven. We don't need to be in a hurry to get to heaven, though, to have a taste of what it will be like. Through our kindness, generosity, and gratitude we all can work to bring more peace to the world, which is the most direct way to bring more peace to our own individual lives.

Reminders and Practices

- Contemplate: Is there something you can do to help someone else have "enough"?

- Acknowledge gifts others give you, be it their time or something you need. Show appreciation and let them know their offering was more than enough.

- There is a particular order of monks who allow themselves only one hundred material objects. Try making a list of the one hundred things you would consider essential if you were such a monk. Do the one hundred items on your list feel like "enough" to you?

- If you see a piece of trash on the ground, please consider picking it up and throwing it away. It's a small but important way of showing God you appreciate His great gift to us.

- Life is grand without the grandstand! Celebrate something simple.

- Say a prayer of thanks for all you have, all God has given you.

12

Young at Heart

You were beautiful then, but you're way more beautiful now.

—James Maddock

———

While I thought that I was learning how to live, I have been learning how to die.

—Leonardo da Vinci

———

Life is a great surprise. I do not see why death shouldn't be an even greater one.

—Vladimir Nabokov

It's been many yesterdays since I was young and cute, but I still think of myself as young and cute. Our thoughts (let's say it together!) are *energy* and they can directly affect our state of wellness, how we age, and even how we look.

We get a lot of crazy mixed messages in the media—on one hand it seems like they want you to think your life is over if you're over thirty; on the other it's like "fifty is the new forty"—either way I'm past their "sell-by" date, but I don't feel bad about it. In my last book I shared one of my best secrets for feeling good about yourself. Every day I look in the mirror and tell myself, "You are *so* beautiful!" When you do that, the positive feelings begin to stay with you and become part of you to the point where you barely have to remind yourself anymore. Since then, I've gotten a lot of great feedback from people who have tried this and told me it's working for them. I love hearing that! But I think for me the best comment is one I heard at one of my bookstore appearances. A woman came up to me afterward and said, "I liked what you said in your book, but it's really hard for me. I don't feel beautiful. I've never thought about myself that way. But even though I didn't really believe it, I wanted to try it. So I told myself, 'Even though I'm not beautiful, today I'm going to pretend I am!'" I really admire that—her willingness to try that even when she had trouble believing it. She needed to put her own twist on it, but she made the effort. I love that she shared that with me, that I'd been able to persuade her, in a sense, that there was a way to feel good and that she was worth making that effort.

Hollywood has a lot of smoke and mirrors. You can't hold yourself to some Angelina Jolie/Catherine Zeta-Jones or George Clooney/Brad Pitt standard. They've got professionals to do their makeup and make them all perfect looking. We need to learn how to be nicer to ourselves, love ourselves, without buying into some media "ideal" of how we should look or be. Even though we're only young once in this body, for the rest of our lives we can use our imaginations. Beneath the skin we each have an inner beauty that can carry us the rest of our lives.

I'm not going to lie. It's a lot easier to make that effort when you are still young. The older we get, the harder it seems it is to change our habits. A lot of times it seems we just don't want to be bothered. Like, after fifty, sex can be like changing the sheets. It's a job you don't really want to do, even though when you finally get around to doing it you're glad you did it.

No joke, the physical plane wears a body down. And most of us have jobs and lifestyles that put the Energizer Bunny to shame. By the time we're in our fourth, fifth, and sixth decades, some of us have been dealing with karmic challenges to our health and general wellness for a very long time and may be getting weary. But I'll tell you what really turns me on. It's seeing someone who is older who just keeps on keeping on. Older people who try to stay vital and healthy are a true inspiration to me. These folks are such great models for anyone of any age. They may not be completely fearless, but they are fierce! They have worked full lives and certainly seen their share of tragedy as well as good times. As we age, it's naturally more likely that we'll have experienced the loss of loved ones—the older we get, the greater the number of our closest and dearest friends who have crossed to the Other Side will be. Human suffering is certainly not unknown to them. Yet these folks choose to fully embrace the gift of life they've been given. They are reservoirs of accumulated wisdom and provide sustaining bonding and support in their individual families and their communities, as well as to any far-flung friends or other members of their Soul Link Group.

Spirit and Energy

Nobody gets into their senior years in good shape without having a close connection with the Other Side. A knowledge of God and spirit is the most sustaining and energizing force there is. A woman came to see me and was telling me about her ninety-year-old uncle, her mother's brother. She loved him; he was in great shape for his age and was just a wonderful man—the life of the party, she told me, and always very sweet and adorable. Since her mother died, she'd been checking up on him.

One day, she went to see him, and when she walked into his home she noticed it was completely cleaned up. This was unusual because he was somewhat untidy and she had often offered to help him clean up, but he always would say, "No, no, you don't have to do that." He'd never allow her to lift a finger. But this time he was sitting there and everything was completely spiffy, organized and polished, and he looked a little bewildered. He was being unusually quiet and she was concerned. She asked him what happened and he said, "Sit down. I want to talk to you a minute." He said he was shocked himself, but the night before he had woken up and there were angels all around him. They asked him to come with them, but he had told them, "No, I really don't want to go yet; I'd really like to stay here for a while more." Finally as he was talking to them he got up out of bed and looked in the mirror and saw himself. He had dark hair again, he was young, he had no body aches—he was seeing himself as a young man as he was talking with these angels. My feeling is that they were trying to let him know that's what he'd look like on the Other Side—"forever thirty." Anyway, he said they told him, "Okay, if you don't want to come now, you don't have to." They were going to leave and he said, "Listen, before you leave, can I please stay this way for a little while?" (Meaning, could he stay young, like they had shown him in the mirror.) And they said, "Okay." He told her there were a few things he thought he'd like to do before he went back to bed. So he then cleaned up his entire house, and what's more, he then went into the backyard and saw some things that needed tending to that he hadn't had the energy or strength to get to, but now he also cleaned up the backyard. He straightened everything up, inside and out, and he even got his coffee ready. He loaded the coffee machine because, he said, he wanted to see in the morning when he woke up if he'd been dreaming. He then went back to bed and lay down and went back to sleep. But the next day when he got up, everything was as it was the night before. Including the coffee dripping down into the carafe all on its own because he'd set it up the night before. He asked his niece not to tell anyone what he was telling her because he knew that due to his age, everyone would just assume he was nuts. She said, "Concetta, could it be true?" I said, "Yes, of course."

We all talk about our energy—our energy level—without considering just how literal this is. It *literally* is the level of energy in our body that determines if we are sick or well, *energized* or depleted, whether our spirit is strongly present in the body or weak, absent from the body. Throughout life, our spirit comes and goes from the body. It may separate from the body in the dream state, during astral travel, when we are sick, or as we age. I believe in older people there is some back-and-forth as they begin to wrap up their earthly business and think about going home—in subconscious states they may be visiting with the spirits of loved ones who have crossed—so it's no wonder that older folks seem to have less energy; their spirit may not be entirely with the physical body, literally giving it its animating vitality. Each of us when we come here has a complement of energy, but all energy originates from the Other Side; it comes from the Holy Spirit, from God.

Getting a Lift

I'm the first person to say that there are things I don't understand. I am not scientifically wired—that's just not one of my gifts this time around—so I could not give you the exact mechanics of how a so-called miracle happens. What I do know is that sometimes we will face an extreme challenge and by some force, usually not possessed by us, we will be able to overcome that challenge, whether it is a matter of recovering from a serious illness or a case of a mother lifting a car off a child. Somehow our body is infused with extra energy. We hear those stories every now and then and we sit back and say to ourselves, "That's amazing." Somehow that soul was sending out a message to the Other Side: "I *need* this!" And they received the fortification they sought.

More often our "energy work" is of a more mundane nature. It's every day making the *choice*, setting out with the conscious *intention*, that we are going to do the best we can with our given circumstances.

A few months ago, I was sick with a sinus infection that was so bad I could hardly breathe. I was still working with clients but I was saying to them, "If you don't want to stay, I understand." I was blowing my nose and sounded so congested. They all said, "Concetta, we're not leaving; we're just glad you didn't cancel us." I said, "All right," and persevered. Now, I could have called and canceled all of them. It would have been legitimate—I was very sick—and I think everyone would have been understanding. But I made the decision that this was something I could do, and I believe that setting that intention earned me some spiritual points and the souls who look after me did all they could to keep me comfortable under circumstances that were not ideal.

I'm not breaking my arm patting myself on the back—I think

this would be the case for any of us. Could I have done the same if I had been stricken with something really terrible? Life threatening? I don't know; I'm certain there is a limit. There is a point where we all have to understand that we can't do any more, though I don't know where the limit is. My keeping my appointments with a serious sinus infection was not a miracle; I was just bringing as much energy to bear as I could to be able to get through something I'd promised. To do that I may have gotten a little extra help from the Other Side, and I believe that when we are doing our best it's not unusual for the Other Side to help us out as much as it can.

Bedside Manner of the Other Side

I must tell you, the dead folks on the Other Side really do care about our staying well and in good shape. Besides the extra occasional energy infusions, I am constantly delivering messages from spirits who want their loved ones to stop behaviors that are ruining their health. You might think a ghost wouldn't care about the body, but they absolutely do. Physical illness, pain, and decline are very real on this side, and besides, when an individual is doing something harmful to themselves, there are often far-ranging negative effects on others in the family—whether psychological or emotional, or even financial if they're trying to handle the costs of treatment, which can cause their loved ones a lot of stress and anxiety. So spirits care deeply about our health. They're always saying, "Tell my son he needs to stop smoking." "Tell my daughters I don't want them drinking away their lives and happiness like I did." They'll also express pleasure when someone they care about does quit a harmful behavior. They'll say, "Please tell him how proud I am of him that he was able to do what I couldn't do." They completely understand how difficult it can be for someone here.

On the Other Side, there is no addiction—the spirit is completely free from wanting. But they know how it is here.

Smoking and drinking aren't the only things they talk about. They may tell me that a client (whom they are watching over) is not taking their medication. Either that person has a prescription and they just don't fill it, or they fill it but don't take their pills. Or the spirit may want me to convey that the person needs to see a doctor to have a prescription changed because there is something else that will be more beneficial to them. In spirit form they are aware of everything, so even if a soul was not any kind of medical expert in the flesh, now they are aware that there is some better treatment for that person to whom they are a guardian. They may also say simply, "Tell them not to push themselves so hard. They're working too hard. It's not good."

Sometimes a spirit will deliver a message that is insisting the person having the reading go for a particular medical test. They may show me that it's a problem with the heart or a problem with the legs—or it could be anything really, maybe something with the blood. Spiritual healing through early detection!

There also are times when a spirit will intervene directly with an injury or illness, placing energy on a sore or sprained muscle, for instance, to aid the body's natural healing processes. Or sometimes if we are very upset about something, they'll put something in front of us that will be calming to us because they know that besides the emotional distress we're in, staying in a stressed-out state is very bad for all the systems of the body.

I was doing a show some years ago after I'd just had a fight with John that morning. I was so angry and beside myself that I didn't know how I was going to perform, how I could calm myself down and be able to listen for dead folks and bring those messages of love and comfort. I really didn't know how I was going to be able to do it. But when I got to the venue, Ginger and I went into the back room and just prayed for ten minutes. I just prayed and asked the Holy Spirit to come into my body and my soul and my mind and help me to put the stress out of my body and separate myself from what was disturbing me so that I could go in there and give these messages. It was simple, but it worked! It was amazing. When I walked in that morning, people who are close to me thought, "How is she going to do this?" And yet, I went into that show and it was a fabulous show. The magic of prayer brought peace to me. It was the prayer, but it was also my choice. I *wanted* that. I told the universe by my very actions of getting to a quiet place and praying that I didn't want to hold on to the anger—I wasn't conflicted about that. I was clearly asking for the healing power of God. I said, "God, I want it." The energy I had going around in me was very confused and chaotic, but the prayer somehow organized the energy and calmed me. I brought a bigger energy than my own to it. My energy was there and completely dysfunctional. But by my clear intentions I brought the energy of God to it, which is the big-guns-in-town energy; I invited it in, I welcomed it, and it came over me like it was a tranquilizer.

It's so funny. People spend the first thirty years of their lives inspecting their bodies for every kind of flaw, then they spend the next thirty years comparing them to how good they used to look. The body is the vehicle through which we learn our lessons on the physical plane, but the soul is eternal and recognizes eternal principles and truths. The body brings us both joy and sadness but knows no constant, only changing sensations and emotions like the weather—any peace we experience is fleeting. The soul knows only pure joy and love. The soul knows no craving, only peace.

Your angels do all they can to guide you, to bring your physical existence into alignment with your eternal soul existence.

Aging Loved Ones

Besides the fact that we all are getting older every day, so is everyone we care about. Our parents, who hopefully have been our role models and cared for us when we were kids, may now need our care. The situation will be different for each of us, but many people will deal with karma in this process or will be learning significant life lessons. We'll have many opportunities for spiritual growth in how we handle any day-to-day details we're responsible for, and opportunities to be both student and teacher. When a loved one crosses, grieving is natural, but my hope is that you will be comforted by knowing that person is still with you in spirit form, walking beside you in all you do.

Dear Concetta,

I'm writing to tell you that I purchased your book, Do Dead People Watch You Shower? *and I LOVE it! I have always been interested in the Other Side and what my friends and family whom have died are doing over there. Thank you so much for sharing your special abilities with us.*

Here is a story I have experienced that I would like to share with you. When I was in junior high school I lost my best friend. I remember going to the funeral and looking at her gorgeous face and long curls in the casket. I would lie in bed at night and see her face for months after. From that day forward, I was always afraid to go to funerals because I did not want to see a dead body again and see their face when trying to sleep. My father passed on about six years ago and I watched him die in the nursing home. He had Alzheimer's so he did not know us. While he was dying, we were by his side comforting him, touching him and telling him it was OK to go and to follow the light. I touched his toes when saying that and his toes wiggled, like he understood me. When he was gone, he looked like the skeleton hanging in the corner of the Science class when you were a kid. I looked at his dead face and I said, "Thank you, Dad." I'm not afraid any more to look at dead bodies. It took 35+ years for me to overcome that fear. What a relief! My sister and I looked at his dead body and said to each other that it doesn't even look like Dad any more. We assumed his soul had already moved on.

My sister and I were at her house trying to figure out what we were going to wear to Dad's memorial. We were going back and forth from her bedroom to her extra bedroom trying to decide what to wear. You know us women, sometimes we can't make a decision on what to wear, go figure! In her extra bedroom the ironing board was set up with some clothes lying over it. One piece of clothing was a sweater of my father's that my sister took home. She went into the extra bedroom to get something and asked me if I was going to wear her light blue crystal bracelet sitting on the sweater on the ironing board. I told her I did not put the bracelet there and asked if she did. She said no. We both looked at each other and said, "DAD!" He must have made it to the Other Side and that was his way of telling us. We both had goose bumps all over our bodies!

Thanks again for sharing your special abilities. GOD bless you!

Nearly all of us will grow old; all of us will eventually die. It's hard for us to see those we love and have known as young and "full of life" succumb to illness or become debilitated. Until we get there ourselves we can't possibly know what they are going through, and we may try to give them advice about what they should eat or what kind of exercise they should do to help them hold on to their vitality, feeling like we have their best interests at heart. Sometimes our advice will really be valuable and appreciated, but we need to balance that carefully. Other than those with a particular form of psychic ability, most are not sensitive enough to actually feel what the other person is feeling. We can't know another's level of discomfort and pain. The human journey is designed so that to varying degrees our physical capabilities decline as we age. We can't see as well as we once could. Our metabolism slows and we can't enjoy all the super-fattening stuff we could eat as kids without paying the price. We may lose teeth and need dentures. We'll have various aches and pains—some of them severe. And so forth. In this way we come to realize how annoying we may have been to another person when we were younger and had all the answers—"You just need to do X and you'll feel so much better!" Now we see that sometimes it isn't that simple. Aging is a great teacher of empathy!

Going Home

When someone dies we frequently hear people say, "God called her home." I admit, this is an idea I myself have considered. But I honestly do not believe this is what happens. From everything I have heard from the Other Side, we ourselves decide to go home when we know it's time. This may sound strange when you think of deaths that seem sudden or meaningless or "tragic" in earth terms. But I do believe at a subconscious level, at a spiritual level, that person knows they have finished what they came here to do this time. It may even be, as we've already discussed, that their death, the lesson it would provide for themselves or others, is the point of their life (and this can be true of a single death or a mass tragedy—a plane crash, a building collapse, a holocaust, even). There is a plan for each of us, one that we devise with God before being born into another life.

I want to share something here that I know will be controversial. Human longevity continues to increase. Over the next ten to twenty years I believe it will become much more common to have an expectation of living as long as 120 years. There are so many medical advances coming—treatments for everything from lupus to MS, to diabetes, to even cancer. I hear it from the Other Side; a lot of progress is being made. I've been told that these diseases will not have the negative power over us that they have had in the past; many, many people will be able to be symptom free, even cured. This is tremendously exciting. And yet the body will still deteriorate over time and this is rarely a pretty picture.

The downside of people living longer is that many will have degenerative conditions, simply the natural symptoms of old age, and it will be a scary time without enough medicine, caregivers, or beds for all. Even now many lives are being prolonged past what they should, past the individual having any quality of life, which does not bring any joy or satisfaction to that individual and places an enormous burden on their family and their caregivers. If someone who is suffering—who cannot even get out of bed, eat for himself, or breathe for himself and has no hope of ever "getting better"—wishes to leave his used-up physical body, I don't believe any religious leader or political leader has the right to forbid or prevent this. They should not have the right to choose for us. Each of us should have the right to choose to go home when there is nothing more we can do here and remaining here is only about pain and suffering for all involved.

In this society, in this particular context, we treat our animals more humanely than we treat our fellow human beings, our families, and loved ones. If our beloved dog or cat is so old and feeble it can't lift itself up or has organ failure or any other condition that is incurable and has led to our pet's complete deterioration, don't we—with great sadness—take him to the vet and grant him the only thing we can, the peace of death? It's absolutely heart-wrenching, but we do it; we consider it necessary, inevitable, *the best thing for him*. We don't want him to suffer. But with our family? We'll give a family member a breathing tube, feed them intravenously, and in the other arm insert an IV drip of morphine that dopes them up enough that they can't feel their pain, can't think, can't recognize anyone or even themselves, and let them linger in a vegetative state and say that *that's* the best thing for them. To me, this is simply inhumane. If I ever am in such a condition, I want the right to choose. I want to be able to say, "Enough. I've had enough. I've done enough. I want to go home now." It may sound strange for someone like me to say this; I do believe that life on earth in a physical body is a sacred gift from God. But the greater gift is our soul, which goes on to eternity and doesn't cease to exist when the physical body dies.

Souls Long United

Oftentimes we see with longtime married couples that when one dies, the other soon follows, even if there was no previous medical condition that would have indicated that this person would die soon. That person was simply ready. We might say they just gave up, or they were tired, or they stopped trying. Often we'll observe they seem to have died from a broken heart. Those of us who reach old age stay because we want to stay, because we have things we still want to do. But at some point we want to go home.

Most often long-married couples are souls who have had many lifetimes together—not necessarily, of course, as husband and wife in each instance. But there can be so much attachment between the souls that once one has crossed, the other has no interest in remaining behind. By this point in their life it's most likely that they've already accomplished whatever lessons or objectives they had for this lifetime (it may be something that the two souls had come to do together), or if not, it will be difficult to do so with the time remaining to them so they will opt to put it off for the next time they're here. Usually this is not decided on a conscious level, but in some cases it may be since the veil begins to thin again at the end of our lives, as it was when we first arrived as newborns.

As Dorothy discovered, there's no place like home, and we're all headed there one day. Meanwhile, it's important to use our energy as wisely and well as we can. Stay healthy, stay beautiful, stay fierce.

At one of my shows I had a really cute little old lady in her eighties who was talking to me. She was so adorable. I had mentioned to her how great she looked in her black stretch pants. She had her little routine down. She made like she was picking a piece of lint off her pants and pretended to examine it while she smiled at me and said, "Thanks. You know, they pick up everything except a rich husband."

God love her!

Reminders and Practices

- If you are feeling stressed, angry, or simply unwell, say a prayer asking for peace to organize the crazy energy within you and help you align yourself with God.

- If you have a health-depleting habit, consider trying to break it. Besides the increased energy and vitality you will experience, your angels will be so glad for you—and would be very happy to help you with this intention.

How to Be an Angel on Earth

With every friend I love who has been taken into the brown bosom of the earth a part of me has been buried there, but their contribution to my being of happiness, strength and understanding remains to sustain me in an altered world.

—Helen Keller

Life's most persistent and urgent question is, "What are you doing for others?"

—Reverend Martin Luther King Jr.

Be kind, for everyone you meet is fighting a hard battle.

—Attributed to Plato

We're used to thinking of guardian angels as being something special and elevated, but the fact is, as I hope everyone has grasped by now, they are ordinary souls—our own loved ones who have crossed, or sometimes other members of our Soul Link Group whom we didn't know in this lifetime but with whom we've spent many other lifetimes. When it's our time to return to earth in another physical body a decision is made as to who will be the one or ones to look after us this time. Once we have crossed and are again in spirit form it may be *our* turn and our decision, our agreement, to be the one to look after someone else—very often a spouse or child we left behind when we crossed. The point I'm trying to make here is that we all are angels at one time or another. It's not uncommon for someone who is dying to see angels around them, and some of these experiences have been described. But what that person may not realize is that in a short time they, too, will be in spirit form and will themselves be an angel. With every kind of craziness and challenge we meet in human form, being an angel tasked with looking after an earthbound soul can be a very tough job. But there's plenty we can do to make it easier on our angels while we simultaneously evolve spiritually.

Ordinary Angels

About sixty years ago in India a little baby girl was born to an ordinary couple; she was their third child. But this one was different— she was born with a beaming smile on her face and would become the great spiritual force and humanitarian (a Mystical Traveler) known as Amma. Amma has said that from the time she was born everything was familiar to her, as she had been on earth many times before. As a child she used to do anything she could for her family and her neighbors—care for the elderly, wash their clothes, console the sick and suffering. She never stopped. Today she has personally hugged many millions of people around the world, founded hospitals that treat the impoverished for free, created education and job opportunities for those who had nothing, built new homes where disasters had destroyed entire towns. And still, every day, she personally consoles, caresses, and embraces any and all she meets. She has been called "God's love in a human body," and nobody who has felt her sweet embrace could ever forget it. Amma certainly is an angel on earth.

I have many spiritual heroes whom I admire, and even though I can't help but appreciate the stories of the great avatars and saints throughout time, my true spiritual heroes are ordinary people. None of them wore a robe or habit or had a glowing ring around their head—at least not on this side of the veil.

My dear friend Ginger Grancagnolo is my faith-in-a-nutshell. She taught me to pray like I never knew I could before. She makes me feel closer to God, understand God, love myself, forgive myself—it is all so hard to do, isn't it? But Ginger makes me try harder. I have learned so much from her.

Ginger brought me back to something I had known deeply but had forgotten and was afraid of. I had never learned how to pray by any religious rulebook. My parents were wonderful, principled people and also quite spiritual, but I had no formal training about God and had a deep mistrust of religion due to the experiences my mother had in a Catholic orphanage. But Ginger taught me that God has always been with me, and she showed me how to find Him again, talk to Him, hear Him, trust Him. I have found a peace within myself that I never knew before.

I feel joy living with God and working for His glory. Ginger, I believe, was sent to me to teach me how to use the tools of love, of God, through prayer. She taught me we have to face our pain, go into it, in order to recover from it. I've always had enormous faith even though I didn't understand everything about how to use it or express it. Ginger took me to another level of understanding. Her ability to verbalize the unknown is beyond my own, so I have learned from her things I could not have put into words on my own. This has enriched my soul and life, forever. Through our discussions and conversations I've learned a practical spirituality for everyday living.

My mother also taught me to be more spiritual. I learned through her example to forgive the people of the cloth who had abused her. I still have a hard time doing that—sometimes it's almost easier to forgive those who have hurt us than it is to forgive those who have hurt someone we love—but I continue to try. Sometimes I think if I'd been her I'd have been angry forever. But my mother never held her mistreatment against God; she chose not to, God bless her. She looked beyond those horrible nuns and priests who were supposed to protect her and instead hung her out to dry, and worse. She smiled and laughed and made lemonade out of lemons. She judged no one different from herself, and even though she was often taken advantage of she gave everyone a chance. If someone mistreated her she'd say that it was their problem, not hers. Her attitude and her choices gave her real enjoyment in her life where another person just as easily could have made different choices and had a different attitude that most would say were justified and understandable, but the end result would still be misery instead of joy. My mother gave to the world freely.

My father was another spiritual hero for me. He accepted everyone and loved everybody, as amazing as that sounds. Whatever he had he gave to anyone who did not have. He shared with everyone and he was a gift from God to me. I've been so blessed in my life to have both of the parents I had.

Whether it's our parents, our friends, a teacher, someone in the neighborhood who just takes an interest in us, or someone we don't even know whom we encounter at some point, we all have angel models in our lives—special people who open our eyes to spiritual principles and the right way to treat others, and teach us the truth about God and heaven. Any of us, at any time, can simply decide to emulate the goodness we've seen in another. We can take on the work of the angels and bring ourselves and the world a little nearer to God.

What Can We Do? Ordinary Stuff.

Everyone has the capacity for angelic behavior. Every interaction between any two or more human beings—words spoken, actions taken—involves an exchange of energy. We can pass positive energy or negative energy and there are karmic results to either transaction. But as we have already discussed, "thinking big" isn't necessary to our spirituality and many small deposits into our karmic bank add up.

Show Compassion

The importance of compassion—being able to feel another's pain and help to soothe it, and simply being kind—is one of the biggest lessons of the Other Side. Unexpressed love is like honey hidden in a rock. Any act of kindness toward another soul is an expression of your love. So, honey, it's up to you to sweeten someone else's day.

This may be as simple as sharing time together with someone who is lonely. Or listening to someone tell you their problem without judgment. If you can help them solve their problem, that's terrific, but often what is most valuable is just lending an uncritical ear. Usually being kind to another person doesn't even cost us anything more than maybe a slight inconvenience. It could be doing something that you personally don't care about but that is meaningful to another person.

A woman came to see me who had had a sister named Linda who had died when only a baby. Every holiday their mother had gone and put flowers on her daughter's grave; it had been forty-seven years so the mother was now quite old, and she told her living daughter that when she died, she wanted her daughter to remember to put flowers on her sister's grave. But the living daughter (my client) said, "Mom, I love you, and I care about you. But I'm not going to continue to put flowers on Linda's grave." They were arguing, she told me. "Concetta," she said, "there was only one little photo I had of my sister—it was from when she was two months old. The photo was in this little frame. The picture was in the living room and it fell to the floor. I couldn't believe that it happened. Was my sister mad at me because I wasn't going to take the flowers to her grave after my mother died?" I told her, "No, I think she was more upset that you were upsetting your mother. She's not mad; you didn't have to do it. She just didn't want you to upset your mother, because your mother was getting very upset." She said, "Well, that makes perfect sense." Really, why upset your mother?

Visit this list of winners of the Nobel Prize for Peace and the Right Livelihood website. Read about some people and organizations who have made a difference in the world and allow yourself to be inspired in your own way:
http://nobelprizes.com/nobel/peace/
http://www.rightlivelihood.org/

Teach

You can be a mentor, a teacher, or a role model of what the Buddhists call "right actions," simply living in an ethical and kind manner. Modeling good behavior, teaching someone a skill, or passing along knowledge is such a gift—you give that person the ability to do something better or to do something they never knew how to do. Knowledge (and understanding) is power—and by this I do not mean the power to manipulate a situation or another person; I mean power to change your life in some way, to take a "next step" or take care of yourself or your family. As a mentor, you actually take someone under your wing, working with them or giving them advice as they learn. Another example of being a mentor is volunteering as a Big Brother or Big Sister—spending quality time with a child, showing them the ropes, sharing things you've learned, or just doing enjoyable things together, and often at the same time helping out a single parent who may just be too overwhelmed to provide these kinds of escapes for a kid. This is really being a guardian angel in the flesh. Maybe we don't view ourselves as having the kind of "people skills" that would make us a good teacher or mentor, but we can still do our best to be a good role model simply by making positive, kind choices in our lives and letting our lives speak for themselves.

Say "Thank You" and "You're Welcome"

John cannot pass a collection outside of ShopRite, be it for the Girl Scouts or Boy Scouts, kids' teams, or anything else without donating money. When he gives a gift he isn't concerned about what it costs, it just has to be perfect for that person. Giving is his very nature. He does a lot for other people and often people seem to think they have to reciprocate in some way. But he once said to me, "You know, some people just don't know how to say 'thank you.' Some people don't know how to be gracious or have gratitude." John always says, "You don't have to buy me anything. Just say 'thank you.'" "Thank you" should always be on the tip of our tongue. Even if we already have the right of way, when a driver stops to allow us to safely cross the street, wave and say those two little words. And when someone does say "thank you," whether it's for a gift or because we held the door for them, we need to say, "You're welcome!" There is such a terrific flow of energy that goes back and forth between two people in this exchange. It's honestly not just a matter of social niceties. Both people get a serious energy boost from it.

Forgive

I'm not Judge Judy and I'm not God. It's not up to me to proclaim anyone's guilt or innocence. I have to process my own trials and do my best to forgive, and I have to seek forgiveness for my own errors. Doing either of these things can lift a big emotional burden from your heart. I know I'm not perfect, but God loves me anyway, just as he loves you anyway, in spite of any imperfections. That's a wonderful thing. Holding anger against anyone only hurts us, and holding on to guilt for things we feel we've done wrong cuts us off from making a correction and getting the love flowing again. We cannot be healed by God until we realize that we need to be healed. Once we are healed we become a witness to His truth.

Care for Our Planet

Blessed, blessed earth, the home we've been given, our school for spiritual perfection—flowers, fields, mountains, streams, oceans, birds, animals! This is such an amazing gift that God has given us and it needs a lot of loving care. We've done so much injury to our beautiful planet. Much work is needed, but the smallest actions are useful and necessary. Can you plant a tree? Can you pick up a piece of trash? Can you refrain from using disposable bottles and cups? Can you ride a bicycle for short trips and leave your car at home? Can you make a donation to a nature or wildlife fund? Can you learn the names of your local birds and trees and teach these to a child?

Pray for Other Souls

There are some who see their work as helping people to have a more peaceful journey here, who teach others to the best of their ability the wisdom of God and share with them the hope, peace, and love of God as they get ready to leave. I refer to myself, and others doing this kind of thing, as a "Lightworker." There are some souls who become earthbound. They can't get through to the Other Side because they don't trust God and they miss the opening. Sometimes this is because they are angry and have unresolved life issues. Sometimes they are a soul that has had difficulties with their lessons and feels unsatisfied in some way. We can help them by praying for God's direct assistance in helping them cross. God is all unconditional love.

Hello Concetta,

I recently came upon your book, Do dead people watch us shower? *Ever since, I have been feeling called to contact you, so here I am.*

As a kid I had a number of experiences with people from the Other Side. At different periods in my adult life I have also had interactions with the Other Side. When 9/11 happened I felt almost

crippled by the magnitude of loss and the depth of energy shifting
that happened around me. At that time I asked the spirits to let me
rest, and I have had minimal connection since then.

In the past year I have had several significant personal losses
and I know my loved ones are near me. Reading your book has
helped me feel more sure of this and has brought me peace. It has
also rekindled a calling that I have felt in the past, but not acted on.
I feel called to reconnect with this tool of spirit communication. But
I don't know how. I feel like my whole life I've been being called,
but don't know where to or why or what I'm being called to even.
I have had other times when I have asked for help and direction,
and I imagine that I've gotten the answers that I needed at the time.

I hope at some point our paths will cross.

Thank you again . . .

Keep the Peace

You know that old saying, "To err is human; to forgive, divine"?
Well, sometimes we can exercise our angel wings simply by letting
things go and not adding to the drama in the world. I definitely
sympathize with anyone who struggles with this. It's one of my
own biggest lessons this lifetime. My husband, John, much prefers
peace. He's my cool water and has been one of my biggest teachers for this. John has such a good heart. He tries to see the good
in all people, always. He does not want to argue.

Years ago I was working as a receptionist in Fairfield, New
Jersey. It was shortly before Christmas and at lunchtime I drove to
the mall to Christmas-shop. I had a white car in those days (as I do
now) and on the highway there was another white car that looked
like mine with the person behind the wheel driving like a maniac

and tailgating a very old beat-up car in front of it. It drove on their back bumper and I guess the driver was giving the other drivers the finger. As the old car turned into the mall, the white car veered off and drove away and I ended up behind the old beat-up car.

As we drove up the ramp the old beat-up car came to a stop right in the middle so there was no way around it and I had to stop, too. An old woman got out of the car and started to walk up to my car. I put down my window thinking she needed help. As she approached me I said, "Are you all right?" With that, she slapped me in the face! She said, "How dare you do that to me?!" I was so shocked. As she started to walk back to her car, I jumped out and grabbed her by her jacket. I could see she was probably my mother's age or older, but I'm ashamed to say, I started to shake her. I couldn't believe what had just happened. Fortunately, before it turned into a very bad scene I came to my senses and got back in my car and everyone drove away.

But that was not the end of it. That evening I got a phone call from the police department telling me that someone was going to press charges against me for hitting her! There had been an old man sitting in the car while this lady slapped me—a witness. Now I was really crazy; I told John, we have a lawyer, we'll go to court. This is not fair!

John said, "Tell them we'll call them right back." Once I hung up John sat next to me on the bed. He said, "Concetta. You are beautiful and young, you are driving a BMW. They are very much older than you, in a beat-up car. You have no witness to prove you were not the tailgater; you have no witness that she came up to your car first. If you go to fight this it is going to take a very long time to get it all out in court. And it will cost money. You will be sick over this for a long time. When you get to court anyone will see the difference between you and them. You will not win. It will have taken a long time, a lot of stress, aggravation, and money."

I asked, "What do you want me to do, John?"

He said, "I want you to call the officer back and ask to speak to the lady, then tell her you are very sorry for the incident, you were having a very bad day." I said, "John, are you nuts? I did nothing wrong!" John said, "If you do that it will all be forgotten in one day; if you do it the other way, it will drag on forever, with lots of heartache for everyone."

I did what John suggested—under protest, I confess. I could see the truth in it and also realized that if I held out for "justice" others would likely be dragged into the mess with me—John, our kids. For the time it went on it would consume our household— and I decided I just didn't want that. John was right. I called. I apologized. The woman replied—almost offhand, "Oh, all right, then." Peace prevailed. Within a few days I had forgotten all about the incident. Peace is not handed to us. We have to want it, choose it, and sometimes hold our nose for it. By that I mean sometimes we have to let another person get by with something without insisting we are right and they are wrong.

I just thank God for forgiving me for when I've been young and stupid and sometimes blind. The point is, I know better. I always have. My angels on earth remind me and the souls on the Other Side remind me. I find many signs to remind me.

Angels All Around Us

In chapter 3 I wrote about my love-at-first-sight encounter with a handicapped girl at the mall. These kinds of angels are everywhere around us as reminders for anyone with eyes to see the beauty of their gift.

I was driving home from my brother's house one sunny Friday afternoon in spring; it was prom season. I passed a house where a mother was taking photos of her son as he was standing in his tux—only this boy was different. He had Down syndrome. His smile was big and proud. His mother was so happy to take photo after photo. I was at a light, so I watched the pair of them with joy. I found myself imagining so many things—his life, the family he belonged to, his friends, other children he had grown up with, and also the abuse he must have faced from time to time—all his struggles, his triumphs. I hear the Other Side all the time, but most of all when I witness this type of gift—these sweet children who help us to pause and think. It is so simple, but it is huge. I drove away being so grateful, so humbled. I was aware I'd just witnessed a super great soul. I said a prayer for him and his family. I thank God for being so great as to send such a sweet messenger to us to help us learn, even if it is just for a moment in our day.

We're All in the Same Boat

Human laws are biased and have lots of flaws. Like maybe a cop stops you and he knows you, or maybe his last name ends in a vowel and so does yours. He can be biased and maybe make things go easier for you, even if you were really at fault. Somebody else wouldn't get such consideration. But with universal law no one gets preferential treatment. It's the same for everybody. And it doesn't matter whether you believe it or not. The sun is going to rise and set—that's the law. It doesn't ask if it's a good time for you; it's just going to happen. We all have our own journey, Soul Contract, and karma—those arrangements and circumstances will make things happen to us individually. But we also have Soul Link Group karma with shared deals and destinies, and beyond our own group we are all one; we're all dealing with the same general reality.

Community is so important. We need to stick together, help one another, take care of each other. This is one thing that many religious organizations do get right. If anyone needs help, everybody lends a hand. If someone is hungry or sick we have to see that they are fed or that they get the necessary care. Or maybe they just require someone to help them out—walk their dog, pick up some groceries—while they are on the mend. We're all one—if there's an old woman who can't rake her leaves, can't a few people go help her? Many hands make light work. Maybe someone just needs help getting their groceries out to their car. Anyone can lend a hand. Maybe you have a friend with kids who never gets a moment to herself; you could offer her a couple hours to watch the kids and let her catch her breath. Maybe all someone requires is a little lightening up—if they're down in the dumps, you can tell them a joke. Doing nice things for other people is extremely rewarding. I know, we're here on the physical plane, where there are a million things that seem to interfere with our good intentions to help one another. We're concerned about time, how we spend our energy. But we actually get energy from giving our energy. And it contributes to our soul's advancement and puts a deposit in our karmic bank. There's a ripple effect outward, but it also comes right back to us. Our community is our world and our community is our family. That means the world is our family. We are all family.

Often, I know, the reason we don't do as much for others as we'd like to is that our time and energy are somewhat finite. But even if it doesn't always seem this way, money is pretty unlimited; even if we have to work for it, it flows among us. And it's useful for many needs. Some may find that this is where they can make a contribution, a charitable donation to a cause they feel strongly about. We hear stories from time to time of how funds have been misused and it can make us cynical, but I'd just like to share something I heard from a friend. She had been put in charge of donating money that had been collected in the restaurant where she worked to a soup kitchen that was feeding the homeless and hungry in her town. Although it had been agreed how the money should be donated, and to whom, afterward, some of her colleagues were concerned and suggesting that maybe she had not been careful enough—how did she know that these people were legit and would use the money properly? But one of her colleagues intervened, an Irish-Catholic woman named Carmel. She told them it's not always possible to know how something you give will be used. It's true, someone may take it for the wrong reasons. We can't control another's motives or behavior. All we can do is know in our heart that we gave for the *right* reasons.

Every day I will meet someone or see something—even on TV—that inspires me, that makes me know that God and his angels are all around me. There are small signs everywhere. If you're going through your day half-asleep you can miss them. But if you practice "awakeness"—awareness—that is, if you simply pay attention instead of sleepwalking through your life, you can't help but notice them. As a human being I occasionally have a bad day and forget this truth that I know with my whole heart. But I've been practicing this long enough that I can pretty much snap myself out of any funk and get back to reading the messages God is constantly sending us.

We're evolving. As I said at the beginning of this book, we are in the process of creating a new world, a better world. The veil is thinning between heaven and earth, and it's really by our own actions and those of millions and millions of other souls making their best efforts that this is coming to be.

Reminders and Practices

- Remember, it's small things that add up to big changes in making the world a better place. A little gesture can change someone's entire day around. Try letting go of needing to be "first in line" at the bank or post office— maybe give your spot to an older person or a mom wrestling her packages and her kids. Let someone else get on the bus first, hold the door, or offer a seat.

- Consider where in your community your talents and skills could make a difference and volunteer—your expertise, your time, or some other asset you feel able to give. Can you deliver lunches to shut-ins for your local Meals on Wheels program? Do you have the time to mentor a child as a Big Brother or Big Sister? Is your blood a type that is especially needed by your local blood bank? Do you feel drawn to help care for the grounds of your local park?

14

Enjoy Life

He deserves Paradise who makes his companions laugh.
—The Koran

Eat, pray, laugh, and love.
—Concetta Bertoldi (with apologies to Elizabeth Gilbert)

So here we are, living together, working together, sharing together the lessons of the physical plane. We all need to find some way to feed ourselves, put a roof over our head, care for our family, make a contribution to the world—while every kind of challenge is thrown in our way like some crazy video game. It's very hard to keep your balance, much less to be always on top and smiling. Believe me. I know. We can think everything is fine, then out of the blue—or so it can seem—our world can be turned upside down. A serious illness or a devastating loss arrives and calls into question everything we believed or held dear. As I'm writing this, my mind is roaming over the losses I've seen over the years in my own family and those of my friends. I'm thinking of stories the TV news has made us all aware of, challenges and losses and cause for tears throughout our community and all around the world. I often find myself out of patience with the media, but this is one thing I will say for it: It does show us that we are not alone in our grief and suffering. No matter what is going on in my little life, there is always, it seems, someone else whose challenge is greater than my own. Someone with whom I can feel connected and toward whom I can feel compassionate. Someone I can reach out to—if only in spirit—and share some tears with.

When we're grieving it's like our soul is missing, and in a real sense it is; it's completely wrapped up in the loved one we've lost—like we're having an out-of-body experience, and not the good kind. Grief is an important part of any life and no one who has a heart will get through life without feeling very sad from time to time. When we live with an open heart it can't help but be broken at some point. It's a necessary human lesson for each of us. But we are not intended to get stuck in that lesson, like repeating the same grade over and over. Even if we do not recall it while we are here, we had to be granted permission to come back to the physical plane. It is something we wanted and chose and we knew in doing so that it would involve mixed conditions, not all of them pleasant, but all of them important. One of our lessons here is learning to choose joy. The Other Side wants us to be happy, but it's always a choice we have to make. Choosing joy is really choosing to believe. I want to do anything possible to relieve people's suffering and convince them that their loved ones are still with them always.

There are lots of psychic mediums and we all work in different ways. We each bring our own personality to the way we talk with the dead and the way we interact with our clients. Personally, I was always the class clown. That's just how I am—I've always had a big personality and enjoyed performing. For someone else it might not work in dealing with someone who is terribly unhappy, who has suffered a great loss. But for me it does. I truly believe that laughter can be the most healing medicine and I am actually very proud that I can help people to laugh again, along with consoling them. This is really what our loved ones on the Other Side want for us, to know peace and joy and to live happy, optimistic lives. Most of the dead folks I've worked with over the years have a great sense of humor and I can assure you, while they take their protective role very seriously, given the choice, most of our guardian angels would also like to be partyin' angels!

Choose Happiness

I do not in any way underestimate the difficulty of this, but each of us needs to recognize that our happiness lies within us and we must make the effort to connect with that even if those around us are dealing poorly with their own unhappiness. This is not a cruelty by any means. It's actually courageous and sets an example that others may choose to follow. Even if someone else is intent on being miserable you can make another choice. It's always a choice.

If you are having difficulty moving into a peaceful and joyful place, try quieting your mind and clearing your heart with a meditation. Sit quietly in a place you find safe and comforting. Breathe deeply and say to yourself the words of the mystic Julian of Norwich: "All is well and all shall be well and all manner of thing shall be well." Repeat this to yourself while you breathe rhythmically, in and out, and believe the truth of it: "All is well and all shall be well and all manner of thing shall be well." On the out breath, let go of any sorrows or worries. On the in breath, let yourself be filled with the knowing that those you care about are with you, that you and they are loved by God. Let yourself feel the joy of knowing this.

You have to try to separate yourself from any negativity. As we've discussed in other chapters, you must simply block this damaging energy with a resistant thought. If there is any negative person you must deal with—maybe they're a family member or someone at your job—when you are away from them, visualize your body cleansing itself, purifying itself of negative energy that doesn't belong to you, and replacing it with positive feelings.

The Other Side is always ready to help us be happy. Its ways are simple and we walk right by its efforts all the time. The spirits may steer us past a gorgeous, blooming hydrangea bush, a beautiful blooming rosebush, begging us to softly stroke the full blossoms, inhale the sweet aroma, allowing our mood to shift into a lighter place. A bird may sing beautifully in the tree—or squabble comically with another bird, making us laugh. We could be walking down the street and see young life of some kind—a child, a squirrel, a baby fawn in the spring with its mother—reminding us of the world's and our own renewal. These are some of the simple ways the Other Side tries to lift our spirits. It may also stir in our mind a memory from childhood that brings a lot of joy and contentment when we think about it. It can leave some sort of "cue" around us, a thing that will spark that memory, and we'll experience the energy that flows through our mind, our body, our soul. There are splashier things, of course—they might just arrange for you to win the lottery one day. It might not be the Powerball. It might only be $258 on some Pick 4 or something, but it doesn't have to be anything more than that to give you a giggle and a good feeling.

When you do notice these things—for instance, on a day when you are feeling especially down and get a phone call from an old friend you haven't heard from in a while and they say, "I was thinking of you and wanted to be sure you were okay"—you need to remember that there is no such thing as a coincidence. "A coincidence is God's way of remaining anonymous." I say that all the time, but you know who said it first? Albert Einstein. Can you believe it? He's a genius! The Other Side is involved in helping us find happiness—it's always hoping that we'll make the choice, when we find it, to take it. We need to learn to take note of the small things in our lives a lot better.

Music

There are many things we can enjoy on this side of the veil, many pleasures of our senses, thrilling adventures, great stories—movies, books, plays. Lots of people love to dance or are moved and uplifted watching a dance performance. One of the most enjoyable things on this planet is music—a universal gift from God, and boy do the dead guys love it! Music's vibrations energize us—it can heal our heart when we are grieving, give us courage when we struggle, lift us up on a hard day, or even bring us a sense of ecstasy. Music has no expiration date. It never dies. We can enjoy music from centuries ago or from decades ago or something written only an hour ago. It is eternal. We use music to get ourselves out of a bad mood, to comfort ourselves, and sometimes just to relax. I can't think of one example of someone who does not appreciate some kind of music. Everyone—whether sick or well, first in their class or the high school dropout, even animals—is soothed by some kind of music.

It also has a way of anchoring our memories. Music can connect us with another soul—hearing a particular song, we might remember a friend or family member who was fond of that song. Or it can remind us of an event in this lifetime or another. I like all kinds of music from different eras—I remember certain parts of my life in the seventies that were more carefree, less stressful, and when music from that time comes on the radio it just makes me remember and, in my mind, maybe even relive those times and puts a smile on my face. A favorite memory of mine is the first concert I ever went to at Madison Square Garden—the Allman Brothers. That was just really cool. I remember the guitars and the smell of marijuana going through the whole place. I can distinctly remember the feel of my jeans and the peace sign that was on the tie-dyed T-shirt I was wearing. I even remember what sandals I wore. All of it is tied up in the music, so hearing those songs makes me feel young again. I like fifties and sixties music because it puts me in a peaceful time in my mind. But I also love country-western music.

And I like music from the Civil War era because it reminds me of a life I believe I once lived. Something about music from the Old South just really turns me on.

John loves classical music, forties music, and doo-wop! And Latin music. He's very eclectic in his musical tastes. He loves so many different types of music. Personally I prefer music that has lyrics to instrumental music because I like a story, especially if it's a love story—with a happy ending. In our CD collection you'll find everything from the Rascals to Dean Martin, Frank Sinatra, Linda Ronstadt, and John's Latin music—Selena (a Mission Entity!) and so many others.

In the old days my friends and I used to go to concerts together; now we play music when we just hang out or at dinner parties. Music is the background to our lives and woven in and out and through the very fabric of our souls.

We humans have a special relationship with music that predates history. All music originates on the Other Side—music has been here as long as we have, and the music of the earth itself (the sound of waves on the beach, of breezes rustling leaves) is way older than us. The dead absolutely love music. They use it all the time to send us messages of their love and to let us know they're here. I've heard more stories than I can count of this kind of thing.

Debbie Casha is one of my best friends. Her mother died at only fifty-nine, when Debbie was around twenty-eight. She has three brothers and one sister, Dolores, the youngest of the siblings, was about nineteen at the time of her mother's death, so Debbie somewhat took over the role of mother to her siblings. When Dolores was just a baby the family used to sing the song "Dolores," which Frank Sinatra had popularized—"How I love the kisses of Dolores, oh I love her, ay, ay, ay!" Debbie said they sang it to her over and over. When Dolores graduated from college, Debbie and her husband, Larry, and Dolores's godmother wanted to take her out to a restaurant to celebrate. They chose the Marlboro Inn in Montclair, New Jersey, where Debbie's and Dolores's parents had been married. When they sat down to eat, that very song came over the loudspeaker—"ay, ay, ay!" Debbie knew that her mother had joined them to celebrate the occasion.

A woman came to see me who had a daughter who was traveling in New Zealand. She told me she'd been a nervous wreck about her daughter traveling because her daughter was a real outdoorsy type of girl—not afraid of anything. She was going to go bungee jumping off the Auckland Harbour Bridge. The woman asked her deceased husband to protect their daughter. She said, "Go on down there and be with her when she does that crazy thing." The next day her daughter called her to tell her about the experience. She said, "Mom, you're not going to believe this, but at the jump-off point on the bridge they had music playing, and when it was my turn to jump, Johnny Cash was playing." Johnny Cash had been her deceased father's favorite singer.

There's a gentleman who has attended a good number of my shows. A doctor, probably in his eighties, he's usually accompanied by his nephew—they always sit way in the back. I'm totally in love with the pair of them. Every time I see him I feel passionate about acknowledging him and speaking with him. His wife has crossed—they'd been married a long time—and I've been able to bring him messages from her that he's validated, even though for a long time he'd never been able to actually speak as he was always overcome with tears. But the last time I saw him was the first time he's been able to talk to me. He cried through the reading, but he kept saying,

"I love you, Concetta, I love you." And I said, "I love you too!" I told him his wife was telling me when she died there was a particular song she loved. It was a song that you don't hear very often but she told me that she just recently had played it for him. It turned out that she was referring to the Johnny Mathis hit "The Twelfth of Never" ("Until the twelfth of never, I'll still be loving you . . .")—he'd had the entire song written out on his wife's tombstone and he told me that he'd just recently heard it on the radio and had known it was her. It was a favorite of theirs that they'd loved to dance to—that's the one thing he said that he missed the most. She told him that they would dance again, but not now. She told him not to be in a hurry to come, but to know that they would dance together on the other side of the veil.

Make a Musical Keepsake

My mother, when she was in good health, used to make mix tapes for us—either stuff that she liked or that she knew we liked. For instance, she made me a cassette of all Civil War–era music that I just love. I have a bunch of these and when I'm thinking of her sometimes I'll get one out and pop it into the tape deck and it just makes me happy.

My girlfriend Donna always tells me that since we've been friends she's thought a lot more about the connection that exists between here and the Other Side—what it means to be here and paying attention to relationships and what really matters, what we'll want to remember—and now little things will pop into her mind. She was telling me that her grandmother and grandfather used to live with her when she was a little kid and she missed them so much and there were so many things that she loved about them. One day she was driving her mother to the doctor's and her mother, in the seat beside her, was singing away to songs on the radio. Something came on, like a Frank Sinatra song, and she said, "I just turned and I looked at her and I thought, 'Wow.' It looked just like my grandmother sitting next to me in the car. I looked at my mother and thought she was so old and thought to myself, 'That's what I should really get her to do—record her singing a song,'" because her mother loved to sing. Like Donna's grandmother, her mother knew all the words to that song, and she thought, "God, I'm gonna miss that so much someday. I think now I'm gonna record her singing a song for me." And she said, "I would've never even thought about doing anything like that if I wasn't friends with you, Concetta." That was a nice tribute and a great idea. Most of us are not professional singers or musicians but that doesn't matter one bit. I'd really encourage anyone do this if you have a loved one who loves to sing or play an instrument. Make a tape of them playing or singing their favorites—it'll be a memory you will cherish and it will bring a lot of happiness.

The spirits have told me that music on the Other Side is way more beautiful than we can ever imagine. They tell me everything over there is highly intensified. Though I always say I'm not in a hurry, that is something that I'm very much looking forward to experiencing. We've got music on *this* side that I think is really beautiful, so I expect to be completely blown away.

Play

Alexander Woollcott, a writer who was a member of Dorothy Parker's famous Algonquin Round Table, once said, "All the things I really like to do are either immoral, illegal, or fattening." I'm not trying to steer anyone into a life of debauchery, crime, and cheesecake, but it's important that we do find things we really like and do them. It's important that we enjoy our lives here, maybe even especially because of how much grief and effort we each will endure on this side of the veil. I can't say it often enough: A human life is a gift from God, and God wants us to be happy. There are innumerable pleasurable indulgences to be found here—not all of them completely sinful.

Play on the physical plane is intended to *rejuvenate* us—bring us back to a child's perspective, letting go of cares for a time. It is supposed to *restore* our energy and allows us to joyfully reconnect with family and friends, recharge our batteries. As usual, it's all about the energy. For each person, the thing that does this for them will be different. It could be sports—either playing or spectating, cheering, celebrating. It could be dancing, going for a drive, having a picnic in the grass, attending a concert, or going to the movies. Some enjoy board games or group party games, like charades. Some find their best restoration in a solo pursuit, like reading or fishing. I love going out to dinner with friends. I also have my girl gang that I love to hang out and do fun things with.

We definitely have our Ya-Ya Sisterhood moments, too. One weekend a bunch of us gathered at Madeline and Steve's house in the Pocono mountains and decided to create a little ceremony together. We each wrote on a piece of paper our wishes and dreams and then made a prayer circle around Mad's *chiminea*. We tossed our papers into the fire and then Ginger led a prayer. As we prayed the fire in the *chiminea* got huge, rising up out of the top of the clay stack! It just went up and down like crazy while Ginger prayed. All weekend we just talked, ate, and laughed together. I hang out with girls who get the whole picture of God and the Other Side. We understand how much we need this perspective and how much we need each other. Usually not all of us can get together at the same time, but we're still all one Girl Power gang—all friends with no hidden agenda. We all love and respect each other, so any time we spend together is good energy, completely restorative.

John and I love nothing more than traveling. Sometimes we have a destination in mind—like going to a particular antiques market to browse and shop—but our favorite way to travel is to choose a country and rent a car and just drive for a couple of weeks without a plan. It's one of the most amazing things to see a new culture (or a very ancient culture that is new to us). I get such a charge out of seeing the different styles of dress and the different architecture, and trying the different foods. We love hearing local musicians playing traditional music that's different from what we'd usually hear at home. And of course we get our share of laughs while on the road.

One time we were out in Colorado taking a train ride from Durango to Silverton. We were in one of the second-class cars where they had a bar. There was a woman attendant on the train and she came up to us and asked, "Can I get you anything?" I said, "Sure, what do you have?" and she told me what was on offer. I said, "Oh, I'd love to have some of that hot cider." She looked at me and said, "Would you like some *spirits* with that hot cider?" I looked at John, who couldn't help smiling, and said, "Honey, if only you knew!"

Another time I was traveling with a couple producer friends, Glenn and Timmy, a gay married couple. As Glenn and I were putting our carry-on luggage in the overhead compartment the flight attendant came up to us and said to Glenn, "Why don't you let me help you with this so your wife can get in her seat?" Glenn looked at her, pointed at Timmy, and said, "*That's* my wife." Then I said to the stewardess, "Yes, I'm just their love child."

God's Best Medicine

Just like with music, there is something about laughing that just draws healing, invigorating energy into us. Again, I'm not a scientist, so I can't explain how and why this works, but it's obvious to all how much better we feel after a good laugh. So much of the restorative power of pure play is tied up in the power of laughter.

I love a good joke so long as it isn't mean-spirited and doesn't hurt anyone. And I'm more than happy to laugh at myself.

Everyone has their own personal style, their own way of accessorizing. I'm known to all my friends as 1-800-RED-LIPS. Ginger actually wrote up this fake business card for me. It has a picture of my face on it. Under the face it says, "Who am I?" (My friends always tease me about my big smile; they make this big smiley face and go, "Who am I?" When we're taking photographs together, instead of saying, "Say cheese!" they'll say, "Do the Concetta!" and they all put on big smiles. One time they even took a photo of me with my trademark big smile and blew it up and copied it to make Concetta masks, and they all met me in our favorite restaurant wearing these masks, like ten Concettas—can you picture it?) Anyway, on this calling card it says that, "Who am I?" and then it says, "For the time of your life with dead people, call: 1-800-RED-LIPS." I love that.

As much as I love to accessorize with all kinds of shiny and sparkly stuff, I really believe the best accessory a woman can have is a ready smile and the ability to laugh at herself. That really goes for anyone, women and men—the ability to laugh at yourself is so very important. It's humbling; it makes others smile. It makes you human.

Cheer a Friend

Everyone needs the healing energy of laughter, but in tough situations a laugh can be hard to muster. Maybe there's someone you care about who is going through a difficult patch who could use a lift in spirits, so to speak. I can't help thinking about Christmas 1978, when my friend Roe had just gotten divorced. She was now a single parent with a little girl (Angela). Roe was so depressed. She certainly didn't feel like celebrating Christmas. She had very little money, but she had to put a tree up for her daughter. One night, a little before Christmas, she called me. It was late, and she was crying. She had decorated the tree, put all the lights and ornaments on it. But as she sat and looked at her hard work—it had taken her hours to do it all by herself—the tree toppled over. I could hear in her voice that she was just done. *Done.*

I ran over to Roe's house with another friend of mine, Terry. We tried to put the tree back together as Roe sat and cried about her life. She was saying stuff like, "I'm all alone, with a small child, no money, no man. And it's Christmas." I said, "Roe, you have to find something to laugh at . . . maybe the tree."

"No," she said, "that won't work. I have so little money to even put anything under it."

This called for drastic measures.

I went upstairs and took my clothes off (I was only in my early twenties then and I had a rockin' body, if I do say so myself). I came downstairs and ran around naked, whooping like an Indian. It worked. She laughed and laughed. To this day, I guarantee you, she has not forgotten that night. That's what friends do for friends. Her happiness was important to me. It was really funny; even when I think of it today, I smile.

Yes, this is the frickin' vale of tears. That's a given for us all. The Other Side has music and dancing, but by golly we can have some fun here, too!

Reminders and Practices

- Create a tape of music you love, or ask to record a loved one singing or playing music. It'll give you so much pleasure, both now and later.

- When you travel, be adventurous (not reckless!). Try something you've never done before and ask that your angels keep an eye on you.

- Throw a potluck dinner—enjoy a warm gathering, good food, and good friends.

- Extend yourself to cheer someone who needs help finding his or her "happy."

- Pray for a joy-filled heart.

Conclusion

All say, "How hard it is that we have to die"—a strange complaint to come from the mouths of people who have had to live.

—Mark Twain

———

And in the end, the love you take is equal to the love you make.

—Paul McCartney

People want to know how the spirits are in all places at once when we're stuck in one place. Like, "If Mom is with my sister in Seattle, how can she be with me in Florida?" When we're here, we're restricted; we can only be in one place at one time. But when we die, we're energy, in all places, like God is in all places at all times. The souls can send a message to many people at once, just like God can. It's like having a contact list on your computer. You can "select all" to send an e-mail to everyone. A soul, too, can "select all" and everyone on the contact list gets the message. That's the ability that they have—to send a heavenly e-mail blast of love from the Other Side.

I have been talking with dead people my entire life. To say it's second nature to me would be an understatement. It's simply my reality, and I believe that anyone who has come to see me has left convinced of their own connection with the spirits of their loved ones. To any skeptic I would say, keep an open mind. If you keep your eyes and heart open I believe you will soon recognize that the evidence is all around you. Yes, you do have guardian angels and they are trying like crazy to help you out with what you need and desire in your life.

Hello . . .

I am currently reading Do Dead People Watch You Shower? *I am absolutely fascinated. I recently learned that the brother of a high school friend just passed "to the other side" as you so put it. I consider myself to have deep unwavering Christian faith although I am not a church-going Christian. I would not necessarily say that I am a skeptic about mediums . . . I just simply don't know if contacting the dead is possible because I do not have that ability. I would like to tell you that I have found great comfort in reading what you have had to say. I am certainly a believer in you, god bless you and thank you again.*

Sometimes we quite literally may get a call from heaven.

At one of my shows I spoke with a woman whose son, Valentino, who was a hemophiliac, had died. He'd had AIDS, which he'd gotten from a blood transfusion. The woman told me she always carried her son's cell phone, which had not been charged since he'd passed away many months before. But while she was at my show, she felt his phone vibrate and she looked at the caller ID to see who was calling her son—on a phone that had not been charged in many months. The number was 000-000. Right away she felt it was her son, calling her on his own cell phone. I must say, *yes*. Indeed. It. Was.

A girl who had lost her mother came to me for a reading. Her mother came through and told me that she had come earlier to her daughter by phone. The girl validated that there had been an occasion when late at night the phone rang, but when she'd picked up the phone there was no voice. She didn't see a number, no caller ID, so she "star 69–ed" the number and her mother's number showed up as the calling party—and her mother had already been departed for an entire year. She had been completely floored by this.

A "call from heaven" does not need to involve the telephone. Sometimes we get a shout-out in a more symbolic way, small urgings through our spiritual GPS, or one of those so-called "coincidences."

For many, birthdays have a way of focusing our attention. For me, my birthday is a little like New Year's except instead of making resolutions, when November rolls around I begin to reflect on my year, what has happened over the last twelve months and what I want to accomplish in the coming months. Now, since I was born in November and my mother crossed in November, that month takes on even more meaning for me.

On the morning of the first of November last year, I'd been thinking about the year ahead and had said a nice prayer along with my meditation, sending out a wish for some of the things I'd been working on to come together, and also a prayer of remembrance for my family members who have crossed, especially my mom. Throughout the day, my mother was much on my mind and that evening as I was walking down my hallway I suddenly, though quite absently (at least it seemed "absent," but I know that I was really "nudged"), found myself opening the closet there and staring into it. My attention was drawn to two boxes sitting on the floor—they'd been there forever and I couldn't remember any more what was in them. Out of curiosity I pulled out the first box and saw it contained some small heart-shaped ceramic boxes. I remembered that I'd had these on my bedroom bureau in my old home in West Orange, New Jersey, but when we'd first moved to our current home it was little more than a cabin. So there was no room to have these decorative pieces sitting around. Later, when John had completely expanded our little home into the fairly large home we have now, I had a different sense of what I wanted to do with the decor and these boxes didn't really fit, so I'd never gone looking for them. I couldn't remember now what, if anything, they contained. I opened the first one and it held just a bunch of small hair barrettes—very unexciting. The second contained several small pieces of paper, but when I looked at them more closely, my breath almost stopped. Lying on top was a page on which, written out in my own hand, were the lyrics to the song "Somewhere over the Rainbow." I don't even remember writing them out, but it was clearly my writing: "And the dreams that you dare to dream really do come true." Underneath that page was the Mass card from when my brother Harold passed away from AIDS. And beneath that was a florist's card from a bouquet I'd received years ago. It read: "Happy Birthday to our beautiful daughter! Love, Mommy and Daddy." It was just the coolest thing, receiving this message from the three of them. There really is no such thing as a coincidence. All three of them, Harold, my mother, and my father, now are on the Other Side, but in that moment all three of them—my entire God Squad—were standing right there with me. I could hear them telling me, "So many opportunities are coming!" I was so excited to get this confirmation of my prayers of that morning. I said, "This is so great! Thank you, guys!"

The Other Side knows what is going on with us here and knows the proper timing for the help it gives us.

A woman named Patty came to see me and told me that her sister-in-law Kim's husband, Raymond, had been sick in the hospital. Patty had gone to the hospital to see him. Raymond was very ill and about to die. Patty told him, "I give you my word, when you are gone, I promise that someday I will take Kim to see that medium, Concetta." She'd been trying to get an appointment for herself a long time before, but my book was full a couple years in advance so she was on my list waiting to hear when she could be scheduled. The day of Raymond's funeral Patty was standing in the parlor when her cell phone rang. It was my office telling her that her number was now up for her to schedule an appointment with me. She had been on my list for over two years. Now, when she needed it to help Kim, it was time.

I had a friend named Doug who'd been in my class from grade school up through high school, but I had not seen or heard from him in forty years. He'd written something so sweet in my yearbook that I never forgot him and many times wished we were still in touch so I could tell him how that sweet thing he had written all those years ago had touched me and affected me in such a positive way. But I had no idea where he was. Well, lo and behold, all those years later, there he is on Facebook talking to me—I really couldn't believe it. Turns out Doug is a scientist now. He's still sweet and kind and has the most amazing memory of the days when we were growing up together. We chatted together for about a month on Facebook and got to know each other all over again. He was very interested in my work as he had never known about my ability when we were kids. Well, as these things happen, his mother died very recently and of course he has been very upset. However, since we reconnected, and before his mother died, he'd gone out and bought my first book and read it. It was no coincidence that we met again when we did. Someone looking after Doug on the Other Side knew his mother was going to pass and he would need help. He told me that since reading my book and speaking with me he now feels differently about death. Douglas—the scientist—now has learned something about the spiritual world. He's full of questions—to be expected with a scientist, I guess. Having knowledge from both this side and the Other Side is always a good thing in my book.

Learn to look for the comfort and reassurance the souls are offering you.

My stepdaughter, Jessica, has a friend named Carla whose father, Carlo, died. He had cancer and his crossing was particularly difficult, which really had distressed Carla. After the funeral the family had gone through his things and Carla had kept a number of her father's belongings, gathered together in a box that she'd put under her bed. But even a month after his passing she still felt such anguish. She kept saying to Jessica, "I just really feel like there's no heaven. My father is gone! I can't feel him anywhere." She really was having a terrible time. Then one night she had a dream (a visit) and her father came to her. He said, "You have to stop saying that there isn't any heaven. There is. I'm home and I'm with my friends" (he named some people who Carla recognized as guys her father used to hang out with). Carla was desperate to keep the connection and said to her father, "When will I see you again?" He replied, "I'm right here," and then vanished. Eventually Carla fell back asleep. The next morning she went to her kitchen to get some coffee and there on the kitchen counter was her father's Mass card, which had certainly not been there the night before—it had been among his other things, in the box under her bed.

My dear friend Rachele Barone, owner of Top of the Park restaurant, recently stopped by my home, bringing me some flowers from her garden. She told me her daughter Susy was coming home from Italy that day, and she was anxious because while Susy was away her dog Isabella, the most loved animal of all time, had to be put down. Susy would be devastated to come home to a lonely house in Isabella's absence. She'd known Isabella's time was coming but couldn't face it, so she'd left her mother with the understanding that Rachele would have to make the decision. Sadly, while Susy was away Isabella could not walk or go outside on her own. With deep sorrow Rachele had Isabella put down.

The previous night Rachele had gone into Susy's room to put her clean clothes on her bed. She'd looked around, taking in the room, seeing that it was ready for her daughter's return. Then that morning she'd gone into the room to put some welcoming flowers on her night table. She couldn't help but notice that on the night table now was a fairly large teddy-bear angel—positioned to face the window. Rachele got nervous because she knew just the night before that teddy-bear angel had not been on that table facing the window. Rachele asked me if I knew what it could have been or meant. It seemed clear to me that Susy's guardian angels had found a way to welcome Susy home, and at the same time express to her that she shouldn't worry about Isabella; she was home in heaven with them, loved and happy.

The Other Side works with us all the time, putting something we need into our hands, sometimes even before we know that we need it, by attracting our attention to something or someone we might have walked right by. We still have free will to choose—do I want to talk with this person? Do I want to do this thing?—but it's our angels on the Other Side who draw our awareness to it. Of course, they can lead a horse to water but can't make it drink—and some people can't see the nose in front of their face, if I may mix a few metaphors. We need to do our part, as well. We need to attend our lives in an awake and aware mode, with an open, optimistic, and loving heart.

We are constantly being shaped spiritually by everything that comes up in our lives. Every experience, every person we meet, every challenge we face shapes us.

What I see as the importance of my work is that I'm here to help folks know the truth, that death is not what they think it is; it's not the "final exit" by any means. It's a passage to the limitless freedom of who we really are meant to be. I hope to be a clear conduit for God, to deliver the messages of loved ones that validate that heaven is real and God is real and is only love. I also hope to become a better person myself through this process because I'm humbled by every person who comes to me and opens their soul to me. I treat each such connection with reverence, because that's what it deserves. I'm so grateful to be this kind of servant.

It's a very common thing as we get older to wonder what more we have to do here, or whether maybe we have done enough and it's time for us to go home. All I can say to this is, don't be in a hurry. As sweet as it is on the Other Side, the earth journey is like no other. It's a great gift to us from God. Many times my own mother told me about a time my father came to her in spirit while she was in a dream state and took her out for a ride, only to leave her at an elevator door saying, "You cannot come now. Not now. Soon enough." She was disappointed; she wanted to go with him. But she was not finished here. She knew that in her heart but needed to hear it from him, too, because she was missing him so much.

About seven years ago a really sweet couple came to see me because their young son Brett had died of cancer. They were very sad, but they told me the validations I gave helped them a great deal. The husband used to call me his angel. I was so honored. Over the next years I saw them many times. Then one time they came and the husband was sick. He was dying; I knew this. Some time later, the wife called my office and spoke to my assistant. She told Elena that her husband had died that Wednesday. On his deathbed, she said, he did not want to leave. But then, finally, at the end, she told Elena, he looked up and said to her, "Do you see them? Do you see Brett? There he is." She said her husband's smile was big and happy. She said he was listening and smiling and then he told her, "You must tell Concetta she is right. You must call on Friday and tell my angel she is right. *Please,*" he begged her, "promise me you will call on Friday!" He would turn and look back at the folks he said were there with them in the room, smiling all the time. She said it was as if he was talking to them and at the same time pleading with her, "Do you see them, do you see Brett? Please call Concetta." Then he said, "Okay." Looking at his wife, he said, "I love you." Then he died. She called us on Friday as she'd promised and told Elena, "Please tell Concetta."

No matter what magazines or the media tell me about who or

what I am, with God-awareness, I know I'm beautiful. I recover, heal, and renew because I have God in me and with me. This is my truth and it is yours as well. I'm not saying that we never stray from God, but we will always be given the chance to return. All our better angels will be doing everything in their power to lead us back onto the path. Trust me, you will be given far more opportunities to come to God than you ever will be given to leave Him. God loves us. And his angels walk among us.

Always.

Much love and many blessings,
Concetta

Acknowledgments

A book like this encompasses so much and could not have been written without a multitude of influences—from those both living and on the Other Side. Over there, they know who they are, so I'll limit my acknowledgments to those who are here.

My sincere thanks to my editor at HarperCollins, May Chen, for putting the polish on this book, and to her assistant, Amanda Bergeron, for keeping all the wheels turning in the right direction. And to the rest of the HarperCollins team—Liate Stehlik, Jennifer Hart, Jean Marie Kelly, Mary Sasso, Emin Mancheril, Kaitlyn Kennedy, and Aja Pollock. I love you all.

Cornelia DiNunzio, a.k.a. Mushy: Can it really be all these years we have loved each other and made it through so many tough times together? It seems like a million lifetimes. You have always been there for me. Thank you. I love you.

Madeline Krawse: My dear friend, I love the memories we're creating—times at the lake, at Top of the Park, in the hot tub, shopping, and at great barbecues. I found you just when I needed it most. I will love you forever.

Stephany Evans: My sweet Texas girl (and literary agent)! I

could not have done any of this without your love and support and talent. Mike said it best when he told me I would never find anyone who works as hard as you do. Please remember always, I love you.

Debra Casha: I treasure all of our years of memories, birthdays, New Year's Eves, and so much more. You have always been a loyal, honest, dear friend. I can never thank you enough for your belief in me and for putting your heart where your mouth is. I love you, dearest friend.

Debra Malanga: I remember the first time I met you, I completely fell in love with you and had to have you in my life. I have not made a mistake in judgment—you are a treasure. I love you.

Ginger Grancagnolo: My tiny girl wonder! You are a huge powerhouse of talent. You have taught me so much. Our lives were meant to be shared, and I am so happy for that. I love you. XXXX.

Jon Cornick: Can it be that so much time has passed since we first met? I greatly treasure our times together. I love you, sweetie; never forget that.

Richard Arlook: From the beginning you believed in me; thank you. There are people who say they will help you and don't . . . then there is you. You said you would and you did. I love you.

Elena Oswald: My sweet Elena baby . . . I still see that sweet face that walked into the door at Abu Garcia—a very lucky day for me. I got a lifelong friend. You treat me like no one else. Your loyalty and love cannot be measured. Thank you, my dear girl, I love you always.

John Bertoldi: My husband, my friend, my partner, my only love, my joy, my everything. Our lives are going way too fast. I wish we could do all the years over again (some of them twice again). We go on vacation together for three weeks, and when we come home and go back to work, I miss you. I miss you till we are together again whenever we are apart. I could not possibly love you more, my darling. Thank you for supporting me in everything I've chosen to do. From where we started, we have come a long way, baby! I love you with all my heart and soul.

Jennifer Pooley: You were the one! The first one to think I had something to offer in writing. I will always be grateful to you and love you with all my heart.

Rachele Barone: My adorable beautiful friend, you have treated me like I was born to your family. Top of the Park in Boonton is my favorite restaurant! I cannot thank you enough for all the tender loving care you give me! I will love you forever, XXXXXXX.

Steve Krawse: My buddy and friend, we share so much time together—no wonder we agree to disagree. I love you.

Charlie Chirico: My darling generous friend, I am so grateful for all the haircuts, extra care, and swimming at your pool (with a private membership). Thank you; I love you.

Top of the Park: Joe, Antonio, Laura, Susy, and Pat. Thank you for feeding me on all those nights I did not want to even boil water, let alone cook. I love you *all* very, very much.

My grandchildren, Alexander, Julia, Carmine, Isabella . . . Grandma Pickle loves you all.

My niece, Bobbie Concetta Ferrell: I am so happy you were born; I love you.

John and Darlene Bertoldi: May you always know how special you are to me. I love you both.

Jessica Franchina: You have brought me such joy by calling me "Mommy." I want you to have the happiness you deserve. My life is happy having you as my daughter; I love you.

Bobby and Choi Ferrell: If you are happy in your life, then I am happy in my life. Your happiness means very much to me. I love you both.

Peter Ferriso, my very beautiful cousin: Thank you for my Marilyn Monroe Personal Property book from the Christie's auction. I love you, Debbie, and the kids, Erica and Conor; God bless our family forever!

Douglas Hamilton: My long-lost friend, you have been so very kind to me and inspired me to feel extra-good about myself and my work; thank you for being a very valued friend. With love.

Last, but by no means least, my deep gratitude to all my clients, fans, and letter writers; thank you for sharing your lives with me. What could I say that would make you all know how very much I appreciate all of your love and trust in me? "Thank you" seems too little. My heart is filled with love for each of you, and I pray that God blesses each and every one of you. With all my love . . .

Concetta

ALSO BY CONCETTA BERTOLDI

DO DEAD PEOPLE WATCH YOU SHOWER?

And Other Questions You've Been All But Dying to Ask a Medium

ISBN 978-0-06-135122-8 (paperback)

New York Times **Bestseller**

"[S]weet, funny, and reassuring . . . What makes [Bertoldi] stand out are her personality and positive energy, which shines throughout. An engaging, life-affirming read."
—*Library Journal*

DO DEAD PEOPLE WALK THEIR DOGS?

Questions You'd Ask a Medium If You Had the Chance

ISBN 978-0-06-170608-0 (paperback)

New York Times **Bestseller**

Do Dead People Walk Their Dogs? is Concetta's second volume of intriguing observations about our beloved deceased. Moving, funny, and fascinating, it will open your eyes to what really comes after life—while offering intimate insights into Concetta's own astonishing life and what her gift has meant to her marriage, her friendships, and the path she was destined to take.

INSIDE THE OTHER SIDE

Soul Contracts, Life Lessons, and How Dead People Help Us, Between Here and Heaven

ISBN 978-0-06-208740-9 (paperback)

In her latest book, Concetta explains the importance of the agreements we make with God before being born into a new physical life; gives advice on coping with life's difficult issues, from relationships to a lack of abundance, to illness and aging, and coping with loss, as well as ways anyone can get more in touch with the Other Side and call on their own angels for help.